Why Dual Language Schooling

Wayne P. Thomas and Virginia P. Collier

DUAL LANGUAGE EDUCATION OF NEW MEXICO
FUENTE PRESS

1309 Fourth St. SW, Suite E
Albuquerque, New Mexico 87102
www.dlenm.org

©2017 by Wayne P. Thomas and Virginia P. Collier

All rights reserved. No part of this book may be reproduced in any form or by any electronic or mechanical means, including information storage and retrieval systems, without permission in writing from the publisher, except by a reviewer, who may quote brief passages in a review, with the exception of reproducible figures, which are identified by the Thomas and Collier copyright line and can be photocopied for educational use only.

Library of Congress Control Number: 2017953708

ISBN 978-0-9843169-8-4

Dedication

"We cannot always build the future for our youth, but we can build our youth for the future."
Franklin D. Roosevelt

"In times of change, learners inherit the earth, while the learned find themselves beautifully equipped to deal with a world that no longer exists."
Eric Hoffer

To all dual language students everywhere:

You are experiencing

a powerful education,

preparing you to inherit an enlightened future

and to create a transformed world.

Table of Contents

Dedication .... *iii*

Foreword .... *ix*

Introduction .... *xi*

Chapter One—Overview: Why Choose Dual Language Schooling? ... *1*

Full Gap Closure and High Academic Achievement *1*

All groups of dual language students score higher
English learners
Gap closure
Legal requirements

Graduating Proficient Bilinguals *4*

Cognitive development
The importance of cognitive development in the student's first language
Additive and subtractive bilingualism
How long does it take to learn a second language?
Language transfer
Transfer of literacy skills
Transfer of literacy skills in 90:10
Transfer of literacy skills in 50:50
Knowledge transfer

A Vehicle for School System Reform *9*

Teaching practices
Cooperative learning
Cognitively stimulating activities
Increasing student engagement and attendance
The power of second language teaching strategies
Switching languages keeps students engaged
Team teaching
Administrative practices
Systemic reform

The Multiple Benefits of Dual Language Schooling *14*

Chapter Two—What Else Do Policy Makers and Families Need to Know?........17

Native English Speakers' Needs........17
Two-way
Reasons for enrolling
State policy decisions
More reasons to enroll

English Learners' Needs........21
Transitional bilingual education
Two-way dual language
Closing the achievement gap
How long?
Problems with pullout
Inclusion
Team teaching and cost-effectiveness
Reducing social isolation
One-way dual language programs for English learners

Hispanic Students' Needs........26

African American Students' Needs........27
Closing the achievement gap
Reasons for success
Bidialectal language acquisition
Dual language innovations in teaching

Students of Other Language Backgrounds........29

Summary........30
Cost-effectiveness
Accountability

Chapter Three—Important Messages for Bilingual Families........31

Learning English........31
"The best age"
Role of first language
How long?

Social and Emotional Support at School........32

Expanding Thinking Skills........33

Bilinguals are smarter
First language and cognitive development
Parents' first language and cognitive development
Raising bilinguals from birth

Parents and Dual Language Schools in the U.S. 35

Parent leadership and advocacy

Conclusion 37

Chapter Four—Understanding Second Language Acquisition in Dual Language Classes 39

First Language Acquisition 39

Birth to age 5
Home dialects
School years
Adults

Second Language Acquisition 40

Natural developmental processes
Stages of acquisition
A nonlinear process
Basic skills approaches do not work well for second language acquisition
Why should this matter to policy makers and families?
Focus on language use
The ideal context for natural language learning

How Long Does It Take to Develop Second Language Proficiency? 45

Social language: 2–5 years
Academic language: 6–9 years

Role of First Language 47

Subject knowledge
Literacy development

Special Messages to Parents on More Language Issues 48

To English-speaking parents in 90:10 programs
How 90:10 works for both student groups
Nonstop cognitive development in first language
Parents' role in cognitive development
Cognitive threshold in first language: Age 12

Age Differences in Second Language Acquisition........................51
- Infants and toddlers: Simultaneous bilinguals
- Preschoolers: Sequential bilinguals
- Ages 5–11
- Adolescents and young adults
- Adults
- Summary

Chapter Five—The Social, Emotional, and Cultural Heart of Dual Language Schooling 55

Social and Cultural Processes..............55
- In dual language classes
- In dual language schools

Examples of Social and Cultural Processes Affecting Education 57
- Escape from war: Southeast Asian refugees
- Emigration from an economically depressed region
- Socioeconomic status
- African American students
- Students with special needs
- Addressing the needs of all students

Conclusion..........64

Chapter Six—Dual Language Programs as a Vehicle for School System Reform...........67

Envisioning Central Administration Coordination in Your School District..........67

Principals as Dual Language Leaders 70

Changes in Teaching Practices 72
- Team teaching
- Innovative teaching

Conclusion..........75

Resources..........77
Figures..........78
References..........79
Index..........85

Foreword

I still remember my first encounter with the work of Drs. Thomas and Collier—*School Effectiveness for Language Minority Students* (1997) and *A National Study of School Effectiveness for Language Minority Students' Long-Term Academic Achievement* (2002). Their research significantly impacted my professional and personal vision for the education of culturally and linguistically diverse students.

Drs. Thomas and Collier were pioneers at a time when so many others prioritized the acquisition of English and discredited any form of bilingualism and bilingual program, claiming that it delayed learning English and made "integration" more difficult. Their work opened the doors to a different paradigm: Students in programs in which the goals are to fully develop two or more languages, one of which is English, typically perform better. This should not come as a surprise, as bilingualism and biliteracy result in superior outcomes academically, socially, culturally, and cognitively (Hopewell & Escamilla, 2014). In addition, biliteracy is a mechanism for equity. Historically, culturally and linguistically diverse students have experienced greater discrimination in schools, as their personal, cultural and linguistic identities have not been recognized and/or valued. These groups of students have had fewer opportunities to draw upon their own cultural and linguistic resources at school. Programs that promote bilingualism and biliteracy create an opportunity to transform these inequities and provide alternative notions of knowledge in which different languages and frames of reference are acknowledged and cherished. These changes are not only a benefit to our students, but to society at large, as they promote the necessary skills to participate in the increasingly globalized communities of our world.

Why Dual Language Schooling presents compelling evidence of the effectiveness of dual language education. In plain terms, the authors address each constituency of our school communities—students, parents, teachers, administrators, and policy makers—and present the reasons for implementing a solid, well-structured and well-equipped dual language program that promises better outcomes for all students—both native and non-native speakers of English. Drs. Thomas and Collier continue to shed light on best practices and positive outcomes for culturally and linguistically diverse learners. This practical and readable book offers families and educators information and solutions for any stage of dual language program planning, from early considerations to beginning implementation. Once again, Drs. Thomas and Collier provide us with research-based principles and practices that could not be timelier or more needed in our schools today.

David G. Nieto, Ph.D.
Executive Director—BUENO Center for Multicultural Education
Assistant Research Professor—University of Colorado Boulder, School of Education

A successful dual language education program begins with a community united in the vision and foundational goals of the program. *Why Dual Language Schooling* provides the justification and foundational research for choosing dual language education for your school or your school community. With this fourth book in their legacy series, Drs. Thomas and Collier share critical knowledge and experience with families, boards of education, administrators, and business and community members who seek to understand the exciting promise of K–12 dual language education.

As a parent, teacher, educational leader, and advocate, I have witnessed the immense benefit dual language education has brought to my family's life. Since enrolling our daughters in dual language education, my wife and I, with the school community's support, have been able to build upon the linguistic and sociocultural capital gifted to us by our families and ancestors. The dual language experience has brightened our family's future and has ensured our daughters' success in school and in life. As bilingual citizens, they are now prepared to utilize their multilingual and multicultural skills to fully contribute and compete in their local and world communities.

Dual language education is the true educational reform model of our time. In order to strengthen and expand this reform model, we need more people who understand and commit to the power and possibilities of dual language education. Will that be you?

¡Adelante!

David Rogers
Executive Director—Dual Language Education of New Mexico

Introduction

This book is written for education policy makers and families.

To policy makers: Those of you who are school board members, superintendents, associate and assistant superintendents, curricular heads of departments, and principals can use this book to understand how dual language education can change your life as an educational leader. This mainstream program, designed for all students, is a solution that resolves many issues that concern school administrators working with diverse student populations. In short form, this book provides the research rationale for why dual language schooling works so well for all students and why it results in innovations for your school district that, in the long run, benefit education policy makers and your school communities.

To families: You have decisions to make regarding the best education for your children. This book explains why dual language classes are the best option for them. Families of different backgrounds have many reasons to consider dual language schooling. Native-English-speaking families should consider dual language to introduce your children to a new language starting in kindergarten so that they can develop deep proficiency in two languages through all the curricular subjects, Grades K–12. Bilingual families, in addition to strengthening the family language, will appreciate the deeper English proficiency that your children will reach through attending dual language classes. Dual language classes provide the opportunity for all students to be schooled together, grade by grade, to teach each other through their two languages and perspectives.

To all readers: Dual language is a distinctive school program that serves all children well, leading to happy students, academic success, and eventual professional success as adults. Read this book and you will understand why your families and your school districts should choose dual language schooling.

Chapter One
Overview—Why Choose Dual Language Schooling?

Your school district is deeply committed to meeting the needs of all of your students. This includes providing school experiences that prepare all students for the adult world of the 21st century. Some students begin school in the U.S. with no proficiency in English. Some have not had the opportunity to attend school before coming to the U.S. Many of the students in your school district may speak more than one language at home, and their primary family language may or may not be English. Many other students are native English speakers of diverse backgrounds and income levels. Dual language schooling meets the needs of all these students and their families, providing rich and stimulating class experiences that greatly enhance schooling. Research shows that all groups are successful in dual language schooling.

Dual language education is the standard curriculum taught through two languages—it is the mainstream. It is not a separate, segregated program. Dual language classes are for all students. Here's how it works.

Full Gap Closure and High Academic Achievement

All groups of dual language students score higher. Many longitudinal research studies have clearly shown that this is the one school program in the United States in which students reach the highest levels of achievement. A longitudinal study is one that follows the same group of students for many years, to see how these students do as they progress from kindergarten through twelfth grade. Students in dual language programs score higher on state and national tests than students who are attending any other type of program. All dual language groups outscore their comparison-group peers not in dual language—including English learners, native English speakers, Latinos, Caucasian Americans, Asian Americans, African Americans, students of low-income background, students identified as qualifying for Title I, and students with special education needs of all categories of exceptionality. Many large-scale studies from all regions of the U.S. have illustrated the long-term high academic achievement of all of these students attending dual language programs (Thomas & Collier, 2012, Chapters 5 & 6).

English learners. Schools in the U.S. are responsible for closing the achievement gap for all student groups, and dual language programs do exactly that. When English learners are tested in English, they usually have the largest gap to close of any student group. But when these students are allowed to continue their studies in their primary language while they are acquiring English, they are equally as successful in reaching grade-level achievement as their English-speaking peers. **Groups of**

students typically take an average of 6 or more years to reach on-grade-level achievement in a second language, so the schooling through their primary language is crucial to success, along with instruction in the second language. That is one of the many reasons why dual language schooling works so well (Collier & Thomas, 2009, Chapter 3).

> Figure 1.1
> **The Most Important Research Findings About Dual Language Education**
>
> - Two-way and one-way dual language programs are superior to transitional bilingual programs and to English-only programs.
> - Dual language programs have the power to reverse much of the negative impact of poverty on English learners' achievement.
> - Only dual language programs consistently close the more difficult second half of English learners' achievement gap.
> - Dual language programs are twice as powerful as either transitional bilingual or English-only programs in closing achievement gaps for English learners.
> - Dual language programs have stronger research support and sounder educational theory than transitional bilingual education or English-only programs.
> - Dual language programs significantly raise test scores for all participating student groups, including native English speakers.
>
> Copyright © 2004-2017, W.P. Thomas & V.P. Collier. All rights reserved.

Gap closure. Figure 1.2, from our research first reported in Thomas and Collier (2012), illustrates closing the achievement gap in Woodburn School District on the Oregon state test. The red line shows native English speakers (not attending dual language classes) making a year's progress each year from third grade through seventh grade. In third grade, the English learners (blue line) and Latinos who are fluent in English (green line) are achieving at lower levels than the native English speakers (red line). But after 7 years of dual language schooling, the English learners and Latinos have made more progress each year in English than the native English speakers not in dual language, and by seventh grade the Latinos and English learners have closed the achievement gap and are on grade level in English.

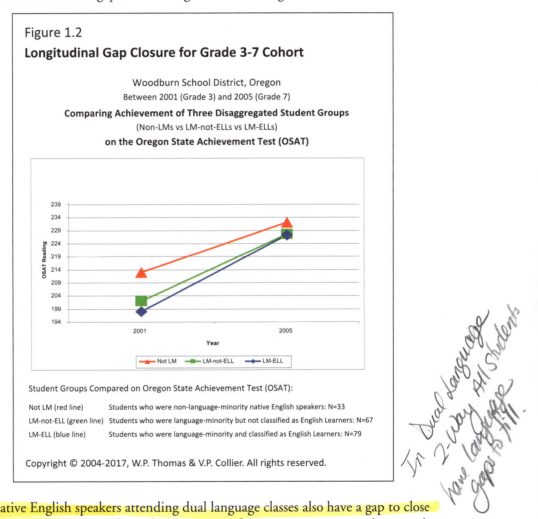

Native English speakers attending dual language classes also have a gap to close in their second language. They take an average of 6 or more years to reach on-grade-level achievement in all curricular subjects in their second language. If some native English speakers enter the dual language classes below grade level in English, within 1 or 2 years these students also typically close the gap in English, and by middle school years they are dramatically above their peers not in dual language (Thomas & Collier, 2014).

Legal requirements. These excellent examples of gap closure illustrate what each school district throughout the U.S. is expected to demonstrate to fulfill legal requirements under *Lau v. Nichols* (1974). This unanimous U.S. Supreme Court decision requires that all school districts provide **a meaningful education** for students who are not proficient in English. In the court cases that have followed this landmark decision, the courts have consistently ruled in favor of providing bilingual schooling for English learners as a legal remedy. Since dual language education is the highest quality form of bilingual schooling, this program does the best job of helping all students reach grade-level achievement. Dual language education also meets the criteria cited in *Castañeda v. Pickard* (1981), another important federal court decision affecting English learners. This decision stipulates that the program must be (1) based on sound educational theory, (2) implemented effectively, and (3) evaluated and judged effective in the teaching of the full curriculum (math, science, social studies, and language arts through English and the other language of instruction). Dual language education also meets legal requirements for historically underserved groups, such as students qualifying for free and reduced lunch. In summary, dual language programs meet the needs of all families and students, while also fulfilling the administrative requirements of the U.S. legal system to provide equal educational opportunity for all students (Collier & Thomas, 2009, Chapter 2).

Graduating Proficient Bilinguals

Cognitive development. There are many reasons for all students to develop at least two languages to a high level of proficiency. The most compelling reasons involve the ongoing cognitive processes that occur in the bilingual brain. In recent years, the U.S. mainstream media have made popular the ongoing neurological research that demonstrates the cognitive advantages that bilinguals and multilinguals have over monolinguals. For example, proficient bilinguals outperform monolinguals in the following areas: creativity, problem solving, divergent thinking, mental flexibility, metalinguistic awareness, visual-spatial skills, and more efficient cognitive/sensory processing. Proficient bilinguals also excel in executive function abilities such as attention to detail, ability to ignore distractions, task switching, working memory, and conflict management. Older bilinguals are more resistant to the onset of dementia and Alzheimer's disease than are monolinguals (Baker, 2011; Bialystok, 2011; Grosjean, 2010; Lyons, 2014; Perry, 2013; Willis, 2012). As this "bilingual brain" research is becoming widely publicized, more and more native-English-speaking parents are also demanding bilingual schooling for their children. They recognize that **the human brain is wired for multilingualism**. When our schools support the development of more than one language, we will see a new generation of students with superior brainpower.

> Figure 1.3
> **The Cognitive Advantages of Being Bilingual**
>
> **Overall, proficient bilinguals outperform monolinguals in:**
> - Creativity
> - Problem Solving
> - Divergent Thinking
> - Mental Flexibility
> - Metalinguistic Awareness
> - Executive Function
>   - attention to detail
>   - ability to ignore distractions
>   - task switching
>   - working memory
>   - conflict management
> - Efficient Cognitive/Sensory Processing
> - Visual-spatial Skills
>
> **Finally, proficient bilinguals are more resistant to the potential onset of dementia and Alzheimer's disease.**
>
> Copyright ©2012-2017, W.P. Thomas and V. P. Collier. All rights reserved.

The importance of cognitive development in the student's first language. For students growing up in a bilingual context, the development of two languages is a complex process that needs to be fully supported by the school. **Continuing non-stop development of each student's first language is essential to cognitive development.** For decades, research on bilinguals has found that if a child's first language development is stopped or slowed before it is completed at young adult level (around age 12), that student may suffer negative cognitive effects and do less well in school. Conversely, students who continue to develop their first language until at least age 12, including learning how to read and write in their first language, will have big cognitive advantages over monolinguals. For example, in U.S. schools, many English learners receiving several years of English-only schooling have been inappropriately

Chapter One: Overview—Why Choose Bilingual Schooling?

identified as needing special education services. Recognizing the crucial role that the student's first language plays in developing the second language and the role that first language plays in facilitating normal cognitive development could significantly reduce this over-identification and misplacement in special education.

Within a dual language program, cognitive development through first language occurs both in school and at home. Parents stimulate cognitive development by using the language(s) they know best with their children to make family decisions and carry out everyday activities such as cooking and cleaning, going places together, and sharing family traditions. Then in school, dual language programs continue to assist students in developing their first language and the second language through oral activities, creative thinking, reading, and writing—through all the subjects of the school curriculum. The accelerated cognitive development from these activities leads to a deeper understanding of, and superior achievement in, the English language as well as the other language and ultimately leads to success in school (Collier & Thomas, 2009, Chapter 4). Language transfer, which will be explained shortly, assists with this process.

Additive and subtractive bilingualism. Another way to view this relationship between first and second languages is to examine the patterns of school achievement for additive and subtractive bilinguals. Many studies worldwide have shown that subtractive bilinguals—those who are gradually losing their first language as they attend schooling only in the second language—do less well in school. In the recent past, the U.S. English-only movement encouraged immigrants to lose their first language as soon as possible. This creates subtractive bilinguals.

On the other hand, additive bilinguals—those who are adding their second language at no cost to their first language—achieve at a higher level than all other students. Dual language programs provide both English learners and native English speakers with the deep level of support needed to become academically proficient bilinguals (Collier & Thomas, 2009, pp. 39-40). In addition, all dual language graduates develop much deeper levels of proficiency in both languages than those students who have studied languages for short periods of time in world language classes in middle and high school. The linguistic goal of a dual language program is for students to be able to use both languages at full proficiency levels in their professional and personal lives as adults.

How long does it take to learn a second language? It takes a lifetime! The process of developing both first and second languages is quite complex—we are always picking up some new aspects of each of our languages. How we do this depends on the contexts in which we use the languages. Since school demands the constant use of our language(s) for many different tasks, it is an ideal place to develop both first and second languages to a deep level of proficiency. Let's examine first language development as an example, while recognizing that this same process happens in second language development in a school's dual language program.

The four language skills of listening, speaking, reading, and writing are developed in school for each age group in Grades K–12, across all curricular subjects. At the same time, the seven language domains of phonology (the pronunciation system), vocabulary, grammar, semantics (meaning), pragmatics (sociolinguistic context), paralinguistics (nonverbal and other extra clues to meaning), and discourse (formal thought patterns) are acquired simultaneously through using the language in spoken and written forms. We develop each of these domains at a more complex level at every age, through using the language for meaningful tasks. During the school years, language is developed even more intensively (Collier & Thomas, 2009, p. 33). Each year, approximately 95% of that year's language learning is subconsciously acquired; only a small percentage of this complex language development is formally taught in language arts classes. **The key to natural language acquisition is to use the languages for meaningful and interesting tasks**, and high-quality dual language schooling does exactly that.

Language transfer. The relationship of the two languages is another key to understanding how language development works. Some people believe that the first language can interfere with a second language, but research has proven the exact opposite. First language serves as an important knowledge base or reference point; it is the key to figuring out a second language. Research in linguistic universals has found many properties in common across all human languages at deep, underlying structural levels (Ellis, 1994). Cummins (1991, 2000) explains language transfer as an "interdependence" or "common underlying proficiency" of languages. He also describes the cognitive development that needs to occur in first language through at least age 12 to be cognitively successful in second language. As stated earlier, language and cognitive development occur simultaneously.

It is natural for beginning English learners to apply structures and patterns from their first language to the second language. But these "positive errors" show that the students are using their first language system to figure out the second language, often subconsciously. With time and experience with the new language and the teacher's facilitation of language development, the English learner gradually catches on to the patterns in English that are the same as or different from the first language. Linguists now consider reliance on first language a very important stage in the process of second language acquisition. **This means that students' first language, including reading and writing (if it is a written language), needs to be developed to a high academic level.** Dual language teachers use intentional and explicit instruction regarding the relationship of the two languages. Thus, dual language classes continue this very important function of first language acquisition started naturally and subconsciously by the family and then develop both languages throughout the students' school years. This leads to much deeper proficiency development in each language than monolingual English-only classes.

Transfer of literacy skills. This positive transfer also occurs for the language skills of reading and writing, across all human languages. Researchers have found that more than half of the skills acquired in learning to read are universal skills, regardless of the form of the written language system. This means that non-Roman-alphabet languages with a very different writing system than English do not pose a problem for students, as long as there is adequate support and instruction around similarities and differences in the languages. Second language literacy acquisition occurs at the same pace, and transfer takes place across the student's two languages (Thonis, 1994).

Transfer of literacy skills in 90:10. This raises the question of when to introduce literacy skills in each language. The 90:10 dual language program model introduces reading in the non-English language in kindergarten, when 90% of the instruction is in the non-English language. All students in the dual language classes will learn to read in the non-English language first, before they learn to read in English. Once instructional time in English is increased in second grade, formal lessons in English literacy are introduced, gradually increasing to 50% of the time in each language by fourth grade and continuing 50:50 throughout the remaining grades. This highly effective model is based on research showing that dual language students need more time to develop the non-English language in the early grades, since they get less support for that language outside of school in the broader society. The English learners need to start schooling in the language that they know best, because it is important that they continue nonstop cognitive development in their home language. Once they are achieving on grade level in their home language, transfer occurs as they develop English, and in the long term they develop deeper English proficiency and get a jump start on schooling in general. When formal English reading is introduced, teachers find that the students have already figured out many aspects of the written system in English; teachers don't need to re-teach the beginning skills of reading. In this 90:10 model, native English speakers also get a jump start in their development of the non-English language, which they need because they get little access to it outside of school (Thomas & Collier, 2012, Chapter 3).

Transfer of literacy skills in 50:50. Other schools may choose the 50:50 dual language program model. In this model, students learn to read and write in both languages beginning in kindergarten. Explicit teaching of listening, speaking, reading, and writing takes place in separate language arts instructional blocks for each of the two languages, through the use of thematic units that connect to the other curricular subjects. Half of the instructional time for all the subjects (math, science, social studies, language arts, and specials, such as physical education, music, art, etc.)

is taught in the partner language and the other half in English. In this model, there are many opportunities from the beginning of the year on to explore similarities and differences between the two languages and transfer knowledge from one language to the other. Beeman and Urow (2013) provide details of "bridging" between the languages, which can occur once students have developed new concepts in one language. Curricular concepts are not repeated in the other language, but expanded upon through a spiraling curriculum. The "bridge" includes exploring similarities and differences between the two languages as well as connecting content area knowledge learned in one language to the other language. This bridging also occurs in the 90:10 program model as instructional time in English is increased.

Knowledge transfer. The common underlying proficiency of a student's two languages extends to much more than just the two language systems. Subject knowledge also transfers from one language to the other. For example, if bilingual high school students take Algebra I in Spanish, they do not need to take the course in English, too. They already know Algebra I and understand the concepts taught. If they take Algebra II in English the next year, the teacher introduces English vocabulary in the initial review classes and they continue into new material without repeating the course previously taken in Spanish. With sufficient bridging throughout the year (or after each unit), their knowledge of the subject can be demonstrated in either language.

There is strong research evidence that academic knowledge, as well as life experiences and cognitive development, transfers from first to second language without requiring repetition of the exact same experience in both languages. In dual language classes, once students have acquired the vocabulary in their second language and applied it to express what they already know, they can succeed academically on tests in either language. This is one of the great advantages of dual language schooling (Collier & Thomas, 2009, p. 38).

A Vehicle for School System Reform

Dual language schooling stimulates systemic school and district change because administrative, curricular, and teaching practices must each be examined and reflected upon by educators to fully understand and embrace how the students' languages and cultures add to the school experience. Ultimately, dual language education leads to innovative and creative ways of addressing the needs of all students in the school system.

Teaching practices: Cooperative learning. Teachers in dual language classes follow the most up-to-date, innovative, and research-based methods of teaching for working with diverse students. This includes minimal lecturing by the teacher. When direct instruction is provided, it is intentional, of short duration, and routines and procedures are modeled and consistent. Cooperative learning is the most important strategy that teachers use in dual language classes, with many varied work groupings, such as pairs, groups of four, learning centers, and whole class. When students work together, the teacher creates groups with varying characteristics, to take advantage of the heterogeneity of the students and the opportunities for students to teach and learn from each other (Kagan, 2013).

Cognitively stimulating activities. Through varied and stimulating learning activities, students in dual language classes work on problem solving, creative projects, and tasks requiring high-level thinking. In addition to this academic and linguistic support, teachers are sensitive to cross-cultural and socioeconomic issues and provide socioemotional support for all. Dual language classes are a natural setting for carefully planned experimentation in teaching (Freeman, Freeman, & Mercuri, 2005; Hamayan, Genesee, & Cloud, 2013). The mix of students with many different strengths and needs within each class leads the teacher to implement differentiated instruction as a model with the whole class, instead of having specialists pulling students out of the class for individualized or small group instruction. Dual language classes function at higher cognitive levels than typical pullout instruction; they do not represent remedial or programmed instruction. Instead, the dual language class is a vehicle for instructional practices that have known power such as cooperative learning and Guided Language Acquisition Design (OCDE Project GLAD®, *www.ocde.us/projectglad*). Teaching through two languages becomes accelerated instruction for all students.

Increasing student engagement and attendance. One of the strongest outcomes of dual language classes is increased student interest, resulting in students' increased motivation to attend all classes and remain engaged with the subjects being studied. Through actively participating in meaningful learning, dual language students keep up with the constant challenge of acquiring their two languages. Historically low-scoring African American students attending dual language classes in North Carolina talk about being in the "honors" class because they perceive this as a gifted program that they are privileged to attend. They are very proud of their second language development, and by the middle school years, they are two grades ahead of their African American peers not in dual language, illustrating the enhanced cognitive development that occurs in studying through two languages (Thomas & Collier, 2012, pp. 112–113; 2014).

The power of second language teaching strategies. Dual language teachers have identified second language strategies they use in all lessons that seem to help native English speakers and English learners who were formerly considered "at risk." Using methods of teaching the content areas through the second language, teachers provide many extra clues to meaning by explaining in multiple ways the concepts of the lesson, the tasks, and the language necessary for the students to successfully participate in the tasks. Students then actively participate, whatever the language of instruction, with intentional and explicit nonverbal and verbal clues to meaning for both content and language provided by the teacher and fellow students. English learners and students who sometimes struggle in a typical English-only classroom need cognitively stimulating, comprehensible, exciting instruction that connects to their life experiences, whereas "watered down" and "scripted" instruction may produce short-term achievement gains but not sustained, long-term gains (Freeman, 2004). In a dual language program, teaching through the two languages becomes accelerated and enriched instruction, leading to dual language students' potential giftedness, expressed through creativity and problem-solving abilities that emerge in their classroom achievements.

Switching languages keeps students engaged. Another important function that dual language classes serve is to address the "saturation point." Many skeptics and well-meaning educators push for more years of English-only instruction, more drills on phonics and grammar points, more memorizing of vocabulary, more homework, more instructional time, or a longer school year. Dual language classroom experiences strongly show that more is not always better! Focusing on interesting and meaningful instruction is much more efficient and productive. When students reach their "saturation point," switching to the other language of instruction often has the effect of renewing student engagement with learning. This does not mean translating or code-switching, but following the dual language guidelines established for separation of the two languages and planned, purposeful opportunities for a focus on language transfer/bridging. Often the switch to the other language occurs naturally through the planned curriculum and program model language allocation; in a dual language class taught by two teachers the switch occurs when the other teacher takes charge of the class (Thomas & Collier, 2012, pp. 115–116). In this way, dual language instruction extends the amount of useful instructional time, leading to greater efficiency and productivity.

Team teaching. Dual language classes are often team taught. That means that each student will be working with at least two teachers, one teacher leading the English portion of the curriculum, and the other teacher guiding the curricular content and instruction in the non-English language. To be cost-effective, these two teachers work with two classes. Which subjects will be taught in each language varies from year to year, according to the school's language and content alignment plan; but over several years of time, students will get equal experiences with each language, across all subject areas. Team teaching requires coordination and planning for both language and content instruction, with resource sharing and creative ideas coming from two different perspectives and personalities, leading to richer experiences in the dual language classes. Teachers often represent a variety of geographic backgrounds, so that over several years' time, students can experience regional variations in the languages and cultures represented in the dual language program, including teachers' awareness and respect for the local varieties spoken by families of the school community.

Administrative practices. School administrators have plenty of challenges to deal with all the time. How does the dual language program influence decisions for administrators? First, **the superintendent, the school board, the central administrative staff, and the principals must provide full financial and administrative resources for the dual language program to succeed.** Hiring proficient bilingual staff and acquiring up-to-date and high-quality curricular materials and library resources in both languages of instruction are essentials that differentiate dual language administrators' tasks from those implementing an English-only curriculum. In addition, dual language teachers need ongoing professional development and regular planning time for coordinating effective team teaching. Evaluation of the program includes thoughtful choices of curricular assessment instruments in **both** languages of the curriculum. In addition, dual language programs add one grade per year, from elementary to middle to high school. This requires another aspect of systemic reform not often found in most school districts—**strong collaboration and planning across all feeder schools and grades**, instead of approaching different age groups as separate, compartmentalized "silos" of instruction (Collier & Thomas, 2014).

> **Figure 1.4**
> **Why Dual Language? The Research Rationale**
> - **Full gap closure and high academic achievement for all students**
> - **Graduating <u>proficient</u> bilinguals**
>   - accelerated cognitive development
>   - additive bilingualism for all students
>   - language and knowledge transfer across the two languages
> - **A vehicle for school system reform**
>   - enrichment for all, rather than remediation
>   - innovative, research-based teaching practices
>   - creative administrative practices
>   - systemic evaluation practices (e.g., focus on K–12 long-term outcomes)
>
> **The two most important outcomes of dual language schooling:**
>   - Increased cognitive development
>   - Higher student engagement
>
> Copyright © 2015-2017, W.P. Thomas and V.P. Collier. All rights reserved.

Systemic reform. These responsibilities of dual language administrators lead to creativity and systemic reform. To address all of these instructional, curricular, and assessment decisions from the perspective of the multiple cultures, languages, and socioeconomic levels represented in a school community results in positive changes in the way that you "do schooling." The contrast between the former remedial ways of addressing the needs of English learners and the present enrichment dual language perspective can be seen by examining administrative goals of these two approaches to schooling. Before, English learners were perceived as a special concern for the school district that needed to be addressed by separating these students and providing them with bilingual and English as a second language (ESL) support. This created additional costs by having to hire extra teachers for these separate classrooms. While segregated from their English-speaking peers, the students saw themselves and their home language and culture as being marginalized in the learning process. This led to the gradual loss of their home language with potentially negative consequences in their cognitive and affective development.

Dual language schooling brings a radical transformation to all of these factors. Students who speak the non-English language are valued and respected as peer experts when the curricular work is in their home language. They come to see the value of acquiring deep proficiency in both their home language and English, and as young adults they begin to see how they can use their proficient bilingualism developed at school as an asset in their professional and personal life as adults. Likewise, the native English speakers are peer experts valued for their contributions to learning. Bringing the students together in an integrated program that benefits all students leads to additive bilingualism for all, high academic achievement, enhanced cognitive development, and cross-cultural, collaborative learning across socioeconomic and ethnic groups.

The Multiple Benefits of Dual Language Schooling

In summary, the research is overwhelmingly clear that receiving schooling through two languages in a well-implemented program is a powerful 21st century innovation in education. Dual language students of all ethnic backgrounds and all socioeconomic classes outscore their peers not in dual language. They master the curriculum better (as measured by standardized and state tests). They master English at deeper proficiency levels (as measured by English proficiency and English language arts tests). They master the non-English language to deep levels of proficiency (as measured by tests in that language). Dual language students fully close the achievement gap in their second language as they move through school. Dual language classes graduate from high school a much higher percentage of students than those attending an all-English curriculum. The average graduation rate in the U.S. for Latino students nationwide is 76%, for White students 87%, and for English learners 60% (National Center for Education Statistics, 2016a). In dual language high school programs developed in Texas, Oregon, and Nebraska, their graduation rates so far are averaging 95 to 100% of the dual language students (Collier & Thomas, 2014, Chapter 7).

In addition to higher student achievement, dual language students have higher self-esteem and confidence, better attendance records, more motivation for schoolwork, and fewer disciplinary referrals. Overall, **the two most important outcomes of dual language programs are higher student cognitive development and stronger student engagement with instruction.** The research results favoring dual language can be astounding, as measured by school tests, attendance, and parent/teacher satisfaction (Lindholm-Leary, 2001; Thomas & Collier, 2012, 2014).

For school administrators and school boards, dual language education addresses the challenging issues of gap closure and equal protection under the law for all students by serving our formerly underserved students well while providing stimulating academic work for mainstream native English speakers. With dual language education, our schools are designed to serve the greater diversity that is ours to affirm and celebrate.

Figure 1.5
Important World Languages

Language	# Native Speakers (Ethnologue, 2017)	# of Countries
Yellow: More than 100M speakers	**Orange:** Top four world languages	**Green:** Spoken in 10 or more countries
1. Mandarin	898 M	14
2. Spanish	437 M	31
3. English	372 M	106
4. Arabic	295 M	57
5. Hindi	260 M	5
6. Bengali	242 M	4
7. Portuguese	219 M	13
8. Russian	154 M	19
9. Japanese	128 M	2
10. Punjabi	93 M	2
11. Javanese	84 M	3
12. Korean	77 M	7
13. German	77 M	27
14. French	76 M	53
15. Telugu	74 M	2

Key: M = Million

Data source: Ethnologue: Languages of the World, 20th Edition, www.ethnologue.com, with permission.

Copyright © 2017, W.P. Thomas and V.P. Collier. All rights reserved.

To be a global citizen, these times call for learning at least two world languages. The current top 15 languages, listed in order by the total number of native speakers, include: Chinese, Spanish, English, Arabic, Hindi, Bengali, Portuguese, Russian, Japanese, Punjabi, Javanese, Korean, German, French, and Telugu (SIL/Ethnologue, 2017, *www.ethnologue.com/statistics/size*). Bilingual/biliterate graduates who are proficient in at least two of these or other world languages have greatly increased their job opportunities and their credentials for additional education. Through working collaboratively with diverse peers throughout their schooling, dual language students develop strong intercommunication skills and cross-cultural understanding. They are prepared for their emerging adult roles in the 21st century.

Chapter Two
What Else Do Policy Makers and Families Need to Know?

Native English Speakers' Needs

Those of you serving as education leaders at the state and local levels are in a position of power to bring this educational innovation into your schools. In the recent past, some school board members, superintendents, and state leaders have chosen to follow their personal belief that schooling only in English is the best choice for our country. These leaders genuinely feel that we do not serve immigrants well when we offer classes in the immigrants' native language, along with classes in English. The English-only movement that surfaced in the late 1970s reinforced this perspective with passion, and voters in three states passed referendums in the 1990s denying English learners the right to schooling in their mother tongue.

However, two of those states, California and Massachusetts, have continued to provide enrichment bilingual schooling in the two decades since the English-only voter initiatives were passed. How could this happen? The native-English-speaking parents spoke up! "Wait a minute, you're going to deny *my* child the right to bilingual schooling?" In the effort to eliminate bilingual schooling for English learners, the native English speakers had not been considered. And in November 2016, California voters said yes to Proposition 58, undoing the requirements of Proposition 227 (the English-only voter referendum of 1998) and paving the way for communities to choose bilingual schooling, including dual language, when desired. Today we estimate that there may be 2,500 or more two-way dual language programs in public schools in the U.S. and many more being developed every year. The website Dual Language Schools (*http://duallanguageschools.org*) lists 1,410 dual language schools that have registered as of 2017, and in many of the states listed we know of double the number identified.

Two-way. What is a two-way bilingual program? This is an integrated model, in which two language groups are schooled together through their two languages. For example, several schools in Los Angeles have a significant number of Korean-speaking students, along with native English speakers. In the two-way program both language groups work together, acquiring all school subjects through both Korean and English. Since the early 1960s, some native-English-speaking families in all regions of the U.S. have chosen to enroll their children in these types of bilingual classes. The majority of these programs are Spanish-English because Spanish speakers are the largest language group among English-learner populations throughout the U.S.

Currently there are also dual language programs taught in English and Arabic, Armenian, Cantonese, Filipino, French, German, Haitian Creole, Hmong, Italian, Japanese, Khmer, Korean, Mandarin Chinese, Polish, Portuguese, Russian, Ukrainian, Urdu, and Vietnamese—and the list of uncommonly taught languages is growing. In addition, dual language programs are provided in the following Indigenous languages of the U.S.: Arapahoe, Cherokee, Crow, Diné (Navajo), Hoopa, Inupiaq, Lakota, Nahuatl, Ojibwe, Passamaquoddy, Shoshone, Ute, and Yurok (U.S. Department of Education, 2015; Center for Applied Linguistics, 2017).

Figure 2.1

Reasons to Enroll in Dual Language Classes

- To become proficient bilinguals in both first language and second language
- To develop a second language at an early age through discovery learning
- To enhance cognitive development
- To increase mastery of the curriculum and raise achievement test scores
- To significantly raise achievement scores for historically low-scoring student groups
- To provide aspects of "gifted education" to students who are already on grade level
- To help students "learn how to learn" so they can cope with faster rates of new available knowledge in the next decades
- To improve motivation and attendance by increasing student engagement with classroom instruction
- To significantly increase high school graduation rates
- To improve students' chances of receiving scholarships for post-high school study
- To prepare students for highly diverse work places and for 21st century global interconnections in all fields of study and work

Copyright © 2017, W.P. Thomas and V.P. Collier. All rights reserved.

Reasons for enrolling. What motivates English-speaking families to enroll their children in these types of bilingual programs? The Internet has probably done more to bring a global perspective to our awareness than any other single influence. These days more and more people feel that we no longer need to remain geographically isolated. Travel to other parts of the world is increasingly available and knowing only English is a huge disadvantage. All aspects of life are being influenced by this global, multilingual perspective—politics, professions, technology, the arts, healing modalities, volunteer services, ecological awareness—the list could go on and on. We are in a new globally connected era.

In response, middle-class parents are demanding that schools introduce languages other than English into the school curriculum at an earlier age. In fact, these parents know that their children need to become deeply proficient in another language, and that is very different from what has been offered in the U.S. school curriculum in the recent past. Introducing a foreign language as a subject during the high school years does not satisfy most parents any more. They know that their children need to acquire an additional language at an earlier age *and* to develop this language to a level at which they can use the language professionally and personally in their adult lives. This is truly a new world that we are living in.

State policy decisions. Interestingly, this new level of awareness has impacted some state policy makers' decision making. At least three states—Delaware, North Carolina, and Utah—have chosen governors or state leaders who have brought this multilingual/global perspective into state policies. For example, the former governor of Utah, Jon Huntsman, supported statewide incentives and resources to encourage Utah school districts to implement bilingual schooling for all. Spanish-English programs were started across the state, as well as Mandarin Chinese, German, French, and Portuguese. The programs include both two-way (for native English and native Spanish speakers) and one-way (for one language group, in this case native English speakers), to deliver the curriculum through English and the other language, with 50% of the instructional time taught in English and 50% in the non-English language (the 50:50 dual language model). Students begin the program in kindergarten and one grade is added each succeeding year. Utah is among the states now offering a Biliteracy Seal with high school diplomas for those students completing program requirements. The governor's perspective is that this will make Utah economically competitive with the rest of the world, producing graduates who are proficient bilinguals and able to interact in the global marketplace. In addition, proficient bilinguals are so in demand in U.S. professions that they are often paid a higher salary for their skills.

> **Figure 2.2**
>
> **States Offering Biliteracy Seals at High School Graduation**
>
> **These states have legislation or other official approval establishing requirements for a Biliteracy Seal to be awarded on a high school diploma:**
>
> - 2011 – California
> - 2012 – New York
> - 2013 – Illinois, Texas
> - 2014 – District of Columbia, Louisiana, Minnesota, New Mexico, Washington
> - 2015 – Hawaii, Indiana, Nevada, North Carolina, Utah, Virginia, Wisconsin
> - 2016 – Arizona, Florida, Georgia, Kansas, Maryland, New Jersey, Oregon, Rhode Island
> - 2017 – Colorado, Connecticut, Ohio
>
> **Under Consideration:**
>
> - Delaware, Iowa, Massachusetts
>
> **Early Stages of Biliteracy Seal Activity:**
>
> - Alabama, Alaska, Arkansas, New Hampshire, Pennsylvania
>
> *Data source: www.sealofbiliteracy.org*
> Copyright © 2017, W.P. Thomas and V.P. Collier. All rights reserved.

Another name is used for the programs in Utah: "dual immersion." The term "immersion" started in Canada as a one-way bilingual program for native English speakers to acquire French. These 90:10 Canadian programs immerse the students in French for 90% of the school day during the first 2 years of schooling (K-1). Then, more instructional time in English is added in each subsequent grade, until curricular work is divided equally between the two languages of instruction by fourth grade. This name "immersion" is now sometimes used in the U.S. to refer to bilingual programs designed *for native English speakers*. It is very important to remember that the 90% immersion experience during the first 2 years is in *the non-English language*. The Utah "dual immersion" experience contrasts with that of Canada, providing equal instructional time in the two languages (50:50) beginning in kindergarten, and integrating the two language groups when the demographics of the school include English learners who speak the non-English language.

More reasons to enroll. Another reason that English-speaking parents are increasingly demanding bilingual schooling for their children is that the process of language acquisition is most challenging while you are acquiring your *second* language. Once you have mastered a second language, you have the skills to apply to a third and a fourth language, with less effort on your part. As parents hear about young children naturally acquiring a second language through inquiry-based learning in math, science, social studies, and language arts, they see it as a huge opportunity not to be missed. The fact is that most of these schools have to use a lottery system for native English speakers' admission into the program, because the schools cannot keep up with the demand for this type of schooling.

Parents also hear about the research results reported in Chapter One. By as early as Grade 3, their children will achieve significantly higher test scores in English than comparable students not in dual language classes. The process of developing two languages leads to the stimulation of cognitive development, so that their children's thinking skills are greatly enhanced. Student attendance is better for dual language classes because the lessons are more stimulating and students don't want to miss the opportunities they are given. Graduates of dual language programs are receiving more scholarship funds and have more choices in admission to university study (Collier & Thomas, 2014).

English Learners' Needs

Transitional bilingual education. By now you have probably noticed that our introductory chapter of this book used the term "dual language education," while this second chapter has added the terms "bilingual schooling" and "dual immersion." Therefore, you may be wondering why there are so many names for this type of program. The history of U.S. bilingual schooling is full of political ups and downs, including name changes to distinguish different program types. When bilingual programs were first developed by federal and state governments in the 1960s and 1970s to serve the needs of English learners, the model was labeled "transitional bilingual education." This form of bilingual schooling was short-term (2 to 3 years), and it separated English learners from their native-English-speaking peers. This is the program that the English-only movement worked to undo. The English-only point of view was that immigrants should learn English first, for mostly political reasons. However, the longitudinal research findings on program effectiveness do not support this position, as we have seen in Chapter One. Instead, the research clearly demonstrates that English learners need to keep up (or catch up if they have missed years of schooling in the past) with mastery of the curriculum through schooling in their native language *while they are learning English.*

The longitudinal research on transitional bilingual education finds that English learners make significant short-term gains while attending the 2- to 3-year program, but not sufficient long-term gains to close the gap in English with native English speakers in the mainstream. However, English learners attending two-way bilingual classes for 6 years (Grades K–5) are able to completely close the gap, reaching grade-level achievement in English and continuing at or above grade level with each succeeding year. Being schooled with native English-speaking peers and continuing the program throughout the elementary school years are two factors that make a very significant difference in English learners' success in school in the two-way program (Thomas & Collier, 2012, pp. 15–18, 49–52).

Two-way dual language. During the 1980s and 1990s, because transitional bilingual programs were being dismantled by the English-only movement, the word "bilingual" became negatively associated with this form of schooling. In the meantime, native English-speaking parents continued to promote two-way schools and the term "dual language" began to be associated with this enrichment model of schooling through two languages. Today "dual language education" is the most commonly used name for bilingual school programs throughout the U.S. that are provided for both English learners and native English speakers. *These two-way dual language programs, when well implemented, have graduated both English learners and native English speakers with the highest test scores of any innovation we have evaluated in U.S. schools. In its effects, the program leads to characteristics of giftedness for many students.*

Closing the achievement gap. Probably the most urgent concern that policy makers want to address when considering English learners' needs is to improve these students' test scores in English. School districts have been penalized for not addressing English learners' needs, but often educators are baffled as to where to start. English learners just beginning to acquire the English language are not required to immediately take the tests in English, but many states hold schools accountable after a very short time period of 1 or 2 years.

California, Illinois, New Mexico, New York, Oregon, and Texas are among the few states that have a Grade 3–5 state accountability measure in Spanish, the most appropriate assessment for Spanish speakers attending dual language programs. When students score high on this test, the Spanish measure is the best predictor that these students will eventually reach grade-level achievement in English. This test in Spanish demonstrates that they are mastering the curricular material for each grade level. At the same time, they are also learning English. Once a student has acquired enough of the second language, subject knowledge can be demonstrated equally well in either language. Thus, measures that are used for accountability should include results from the curricular tests in the non-English language.

In states where there is no state-mandated accountability measure in Spanish, some districts have decided to use norm-referenced curricular tests in Spanish (not language proficiency tests), to demonstrate students' grade-level achievement. We are focusing on Spanish speakers in these examples because they are the largest language group in U.S. schools, representing 77% of the total number of students of non-English-speaking background (National Center for Education Statistics, 2016b), but similar measures could be used for other language groups. For example, the state of New York currently provides assessments for English learners in Chinese, Haitian Creole, Korean, Russian, and Spanish.

How long? Why do the curricular tests in Spanish and other languages help to solve the accountability issues? It's important to understand that it takes an average of *6 years* for groups of students to reach grade-level achievement in their second language. This is true for both the native English speakers acquiring Spanish as well as the native Spanish speakers acquiring English. *English learners who have not experienced cognitive/academic development in their first language rarely reach grade-level achievement in their second language. Long-term dual language programs (at least K–8, and preferably K–12) completely close the gap and keep it closed in the secondary years* (Collier & Thomas, 2009; Thomas & Collier, 2012).

Problems with pullout. Instructional strategies used in the last several decades to serve students who are struggling with their academic work include hiring specialists (often with federal funds) who provide extra support. These specialists pull students from their classroom instruction to resolve "problems" that teachers identify as they work with individual students. Reading interventions, special education, pullout English as a Second Language (ESL) instruction, speech therapy, Title I services, gifted instruction, and other pullout services have, for over a half century, been used in U.S. schools for English learners and other students with special needs. And yet teachers often report that these pullout instructional services seriously interrupt the curricular work that their students are engaged in. While the students are gone from their assigned classroom, they lose ground on the curricular material being covered by the teacher who knows the students best. The specialist who pulls the students out may or may not be someone the students trust. The lesson is often focused on low-level, short-term goals in curricular material that may be unrelated to students' classroom studies. Additionally, social relations with the students' peers are disturbed, sometimes leading to discriminatory behaviors or social isolation when they return to their original classroom.

Inclusion. The fields of special education and ESL have worked hard to implement inclusion strategies for team teaching, but the two teachers in a team (e.g., an ESL and a mainstream teacher) need to be given lots of planning time to prepare and coordinate effective lessons. Team teaching may also require much more funding for extra teachers when one specialist is being added to address the needs of as few as four or five students in a given classroom. When you multiply that by the total number of classrooms in the district, in a short time you have a very expensive program. The issues surrounding pullout instruction are indeed complex and can be politically charged.

So how in the world can schools solve these problems when addressing English learners' needs? This challenge highlights one of the major advantages of two-way dual language schooling. *If the dual language program is implemented effectively, English learners are no longer isolated from their classroom peers and pullout instruction is not needed.*

Figure 2.3

Advantages of Dual Language Inclusion

- English learners are included in mainstream instruction and not socially isolated from their classroom peers.
- Dual language teachers use innovative and effective second language teaching strategies (e.g., lots of extra clues to meaning) to better meet the instructional needs of both English learners and native English speakers.
- Research-tested instructional strategies such as cooperative learning enable diverse students to help and learn directly from one another.
- Dual language students experience a greater cognitive range and a higher overall cognitive level, both leading to higher long-term achievement.
- Both language groups are equally challenged in their second languages and can identify with each other instructionally and emotionally.
- Both language groups can be "experts" when the instructional lesson is in their home language (at least 50% of the time).
- Friendships can develop across language and social class barriers.
- Students can receive sociocultural comfort from teachers trained to understand and meet their needs.

Copyright © 2017, W.P. Thomas and V.P. Collier. All rights reserved.

Team teaching and cost-effectiveness. When team teaching is used for dual language classes, costs can be greatly reduced if the two teachers work with two classes, thereby keeping the same teacher-student ratio that already exists in the school. For example, two dual language teachers are assigned to two fourth-grade classes, one providing instruction in English to one class while the other teaches in the non-English language. The two classes alternate between the two teachers, with different material covered by each teacher. Both teachers are fully trained in second language teaching strategies, and they are prepared to design cognitively challenging lessons that skillfully address the needs of both the second language learners and the native speakers in their classrooms. As a result, pullout services may no longer be needed.

Reducing social isolation. Dual language is a powerful instructional solution to the challenge of developing cross-cultural competence. One of the largest current problems in U.S. schools is that English learners are frequently socially isolated. They can be looked down upon, discriminated against, bullied, and teased for their different behaviors and language. The two-way classroom levels the playing field. Native English speakers are equally challenged when they are thrown into a classroom context where they initially don't know the language. Suddenly their Spanish-speaking peers are the experts during the Spanish instructional time. The two language groups come to value each other for support. Friendships form across language barriers and social class. *When students work together across the curricular years, they become young adults who are prepared for cooperative and creative sharing of ideas in the diverse workplaces of the 21st century.*

The school community benefits, too. As dual language educator Erin Bostick Mason states:

> While some communities look at dual language education primarily as a means to prepare students for college and career, there are many neighborhoods where the ability to communicate across languages and cultures unlocks daily access to curriculum and instruction, as well as ground-breaking friendships among children and families that cross traditional community boundaries. The ability to speak one another's language creates relationships between children that reshape their sense of identity and builds bonds one family at a time. Dual language education can prevent the cultural conflicts and linguistic isolation that fuel stereotypes, gang violence, and xenophobia. (Collier & Thomas, 2014, p. 1)

One-way dual language programs for English learners. We have now made a strong case for two-way programs that integrate native English speakers with English learners, but what about demographic contexts where there are very few native English speakers? For instance, there are many school districts along the border with Mexico in which the large majority of students are English learners. Elsewhere, schools that serve urban neighborhoods can also be defined by housing patterns that strongly segregate groups from each other by ethnicity, language, or socioeconomic class.

We introduced the term "one-way" earlier in this chapter, explaining that this refers to one language group being schooled through two languages. We applied this term to one-way programs for native English speakers. Now let's think about how this type of program can benefit English learners who have little access to native-English-speaking peers. For example, in the state of Texas there are many one-way dual language programs for Spanish speakers, located in schools where communities are mostly Spanish-speaking or bilingual. Typically, in any given school or school district with a large majority of students of Latino background, some students are just beginning to acquire the English language, some are being raised bilingually and are quite fluent orally in English and Spanish, and others have lost their heritage language and know only English. We classify the dual language program that serves these Latino students as a one-way program. They are culturally and linguistically of Hispanic/Latino heritage, but they have different language and academic needs. In dual language classes, these groups of Latino students assist each other with mastery of the curriculum through their two languages.

The dual language teachers in one-way programs must be equally well trained in second language teaching strategies and prepared to teach cognitively challenging lessons that address the needs of all the students in the class, just as in a two-way class. Sometimes these classes are taught by one teacher who is a proficient bilingual, able to teach the full curriculum through both languages, and others are team taught. However, we recommend team teaching as the best model for consistent and successful dual language classes because each teacher can then present instruction in their "best" language.

Hispanic Students' Needs

One-way and two-way dual language programs also address closing the achievement gap for students who are classified as proficient in English but are not doing so well in school. Nationally the average high school graduation rate for Latino students is currently 76%. In the past, these students have often been classified as an "at risk" group needing extra support in school to help them close the achievement gap with White students. Now in dual language programs, they are reaching grade-level achievement in English, and at the same time reconnecting to their heritage language. By developing deep academic proficiency in both Spanish and English, their test scores are going up in both languages, and they are accelerating their rates of graduation and university entry.

Closure of the achievement gap for Latino students is illustrated in the research figure from our longitudinal research in Woodburn School District in Oregon (see

Figure 1.2). In the dual language program, the Latinos made more progress each year on the tests in English when they received only a half day of instruction in English in comparison to the native English speakers who received all their instruction in English. This illustrates the power of dual language programs to accelerate cognitive development and increase student engagement with instruction. Another dual language high school program in Omaha, Nebraska, has had great success with first-generation Latino immigrants. To attend the dual language program, these students sign a contract that they will not be involved with any gang, drug, or other criminal behaviors. They are given extra support for preparing for university study and scholarship applications, and to date they have graduated 100% of their students (Collier & Thomas, 2014, Chapter 7).

African American Students' Needs

In our longitudinal research, we have uncovered what we think is astonishing news for school leaders. African American students who attend two-way dual language classes typically greatly outscore their peers not in dual language. This is especially true for groups of historically low-scoring African American students who are of low-income background. They are more engaged with classroom activities; their attendance is better; there are fewer behavioral referrals; and they say *school is much more interesting!* We are intrigued with these consistent findings. We interpret them to mean that the second language teaching strategies that dual language teachers use with English learners also significantly improve student success for all ethnic groups who attend these classes, including Title I students and low-scoring native English speakers.

Closing the achievement gap. In our analyses of data from Houston Independent School District, Texas, we found that in the inner city, the African American students of low-income background attending two-way dual language classes were significantly outperforming their peers not in dual language. On two very difficult norm-referenced tests (*Stanford* and *Aprenda*) measuring grade-level skills across the curriculum, these African American students were scoring above grade level in both English and Spanish by fifth grade (Thomas & Collier, 2002). More recently, we have analyzed statewide data from North Carolina, comparing the performance of English learners, Hispanics, African Americans, and Caucasian Americans in two-way dual language classes with their peers not in dual language. By the middle school years, both African American and Latino students in dual language were closing the gap with Caucasian American students on the state assessment measures in Reading and Mathematics, with African Americans in dual language scoring *two grades* above their African American peers not in dual language. This is phenomenal achievement that is attributable to well-implemented dual language programs (Thomas & Collier, 2009, 2014; Thomas, Collier, & Collier, 2010).

Reasons for success. What could be the reasons for such successful outcomes? We asked teachers and principals and the students themselves. The students clearly feel that they have enrolled in a gifted or honors program. They are very proud to participate, and they show it by their increased attendance records. They also feel that the teaching is no longer "dumbed down." They have a lot to keep up with, having to figure out their subjects being taught in the non-English language and constantly picking up new vocabulary in both languages, so they pay closer attention to what is being taught in both languages. The cross-cultural lessons help the students reflect on their own identity, viewing diversity as a celebration of multiple ways of living life and solving problems. Through their exploration of Latin American peoples and geography, the African American students notice that multiple ethnicities exist throughout the Americas, and they come to affirm their own heritage.

Bidialectal language acquisition. The students also begin to grasp how languages function, as they pick up new ways of expressing things. This leads to the African American students' reflection on their own bidialectalism, often present in their home and community. They become metalinguistically aware at a much younger age, paying more attention to the standard English spoken at school and noticing the differences with their community varieties of English. In many ways they are becoming trilingual, and this subconsciously influences their language acquisition process, stimulating deeper proficiency in both Spanish and "school" English, while increasing appreciation of their home varieties of English.

Dual language innovations in teaching. Most amazing is the finding that dual language teachers are more innovative and aware of how to differentiate instruction to meet more of their students' needs, without sending the students off to pullout support. Many different types of programs, funded by federal Title I funds, have been developed to raise African American students' test scores in schools that serve low-income neighborhoods. These instructional strategies often add specialists who work with the students in small groups or one-on-one. For example, in language arts they might help students catch on to details of spelling, grammar, and punctuation in reading and writing tasks. Students may politely work with the specialists and aides, but they may have little interest in the material being covered. Often the work is focused almost exclusively on short-term goals and low-level skills.

In contrast, a dual language class is full of extra clues to meaning. Teachers know that they always have second language learners among their students, so they do lots of mime, nonverbal gestures, pictures, drawings, graphic organizers, anchor charts, songs, chants, acting, movement—whatever it takes to get across the "what, how, and why" of lessons. Teachers plan for intentional, integrated instruction to help make both language and content accessible to their students. Classes always use cooperative learning strategies to pair and group students in varying ways so that all students take leadership roles and support each other as they figure out the work in the two languages. These instructional strategies seem to work well with the diversity that is always present in dual language classes. Students of many ethnicities and varying socioeconomic backgrounds flourish in this teaching style, and it shows in their test scores.

Students of Other Language Backgrounds

An ongoing dilemma for dual language educators is finding ways to serve as many of the language groups as possible in each school district. When transitional bilingual education was developed in the 1970s, a common formula used for determining the feasibility of providing a program in a given language was to provide bilingual services if there were at least 20 students of one language background in one grade, or sometimes two adjacent grades. This is still used as a formula for some states that require transitional bilingual schooling. But most urban school districts in the U.S. enroll many language groups, the larger school districts typically reporting over 100 languages represented among their student population. Many of these students live in neighborhoods throughout the district, making it difficult to provide bilingual services when only a few speakers of each language are attending a school; but at a minimum, all English learners must receive ESL services.

Some of these families may request to enroll their children in the Spanish-English dual language program. Their rationale is that they want their students to become trilingual, given that Spanish is the second largest language of the world. (When counting only native speakers, Mandarin Chinese is the largest language of the world, Spanish is second, and English is third [*Ethnologue*, 2017, *www.ethnologue.com/statistics/size*].) These families are advised to continue to use their home language and to provide for their children to acquire literacy in their home language, if it is a written language. Then these children receive schooling in their second and third languages, English and Spanish. These students of non-Spanish-speaking background may represent approximately 5 to 10% of the students in the dual language classes. With time, these students are also very successful, reaching grade-level achievement in English.

Families of Indigenous background from Latin America who have emigrated to the U.S. also have to make decisions regarding the languages for their children's schooling. In school districts such as Woodburn, Oregon, and Elgin, Illinois, many of these students from Mexico and Guatemala who speak Indigenous languages choose to enroll in the dual language Spanish-English classes. The children may continue to speak their parents' Indigenous native language at home, while at school they study through Spanish and English. Some have already received some schooling in Spanish before they emigrated to the U.S. Indigenous students do much better in the dual language program than when they are schooled only through English (Aikio-Puoskari, 2009; Francis & Reyhner, 2002; McCarty, 2009; McCarty, Romero, & Zepeda, 2006).

Summary

Cost-effectiveness. Dual language programs resolve many issues that school leaders are concerned about. This program is the curricular mainstream, taught through two languages. For that reason, dual language is the most cost-effective program for English learners because it eliminates the need for extra specialists. All dual language teachers are certified mainstream teachers well trained in second language teaching strategies, whether teaching in English (ESL and content-licensed for the age group) or in the other instructional language (e.g., bilingually endorsed in the partner language and content-licensed for the age group). The additional costs occur mainly in the program startup phase for curricular materials in the second language and for ongoing professional development. Long-term operational costs are similar to those of the monolingual mainstream.

Accountability. Dual language programs help all ethnic groups close their achievement gaps on local and state-mandated assessment measures. Attendance and graduation rates are dramatically higher for all groups of students. This program has a very positive impact on students who come from poverty, raising their test scores, too. Even students with special needs who choose dual language classes score higher than their peers not in dual language (Thomas & Collier, 2014). All of the groups considered "at risk" benefit greatly from dual language classes, raising the test scores of their schools and the whole school district. This program is a win-win for school leaders and for the entire school community.

Chapter Three
Important Messages for Bilingual Families

Learning English

We know that all of you parents are eager for your children to have a full command of English. You want your children to be successful in their adult lives. Understanding, speaking, reading, and writing English well is our schools' goal for all of our students. That's why we recommend dual language education for our schools. By participating in this program, your children will learn English better and be prepared for a wide variety of professions while also developing the language of the home and family. Once you understand and experience how this type of school program works, we hope that you will become an advocate and help other parents to understand.

"The best age." Let's take a quick look at some of the natural influences on second language learning in school. Recent language acquisition research has uncovered many myths regarding how people learn languages. Myths are things we think we know and we tell others, but the truth is quite different. For example, it is a myth that young children are the fastest at learning a second language. Young children are willing, often eager, and less inhibited learners than older students. *The truth is that adolescents and young adults who have attended school and are on grade level in their first language are more efficient language learners than young children.* But people of all ages can learn a new language. In the next chapter, we will examine how we can enhance language learning in school for students of all ages.

Role of first language. Another common myth centers on the role of the first language. Many people say that their first language "interferes with" and causes errors in the second language. *The truth is that your children's first language is the most important tool they have to figure out the second language.* The evidence of influence from the first language is a good sign that their brains are working the way they are supposed to. Your children need to continue developing their first language until at least young adulthood. If they learn to read and write their first language (if it is a written language), they will be several grades ahead of the students who have not done this (Collier & Thomas, 1989; Thomas & Collier, 2002, 2014). They must develop thinking skills in their first language throughout their life. *Students who do not develop cognitively in their first language until at least age 12 do less well in school.* This normal cognitive development in the first language is the most important factor influencing success in the second language. It also is the most important reason for your children to participate in a dual language program.

How long? Another commonly heard myth is that children can learn a second language really quickly. Some parents talk about their children picking it up in just a few months! But when parents say this, they are actually only referring to some aspects of social language. It seems quick because young children often sound like native speakers, with little accent. How long does it really take? What is the truth?

School and work are two very demanding contexts of language use. In school, it takes groups of students *an average of 6 years* to reach full proficiency in their second language, as measured by school assessments. The tests in English are comparing your children's subject knowledge to that of native English speakers of their same age, who are also growing in their knowledge and making one year's progress every year. That is why schooling in your children's first language is so important, to continue learning all the content area subjects while they are also learning English. If your children don't receive schooling in both languages, it will be much more difficult for them to graduate from high school on par with their English-speaking peers.

By fifth grade, students who are schooled in the two languages tend to score higher in all their subjects than the students schooled only in English. *By eighth grade, bilingually schooled students score dramatically higher on tests than their peers not in dual language classes.* There are huge cognitive and academic advantages to dual language schooling, and your children will become deeply proficient in both English and their first language.

Social and Emotional Support at School

Another very big influence on your children's learning of English and the school subjects is the kind of support they receive at school. At home your activities tend to be heart-centered. As you choose everything that you do at home with your children, taking care of each other and other expressions of love are very important and take many forms. School can be quite different. Children are figuring out their social relationships with each other, and they have a lot to learn. Treating each other with respect, kindness, honesty, sincerity, and heartfelt support is a goal that all teachers strive to facilitate. But students have had many different life experiences, and it is not easy to get along with everyone.

How can schools solve this complex issue? Dual language classes are often taught by two teachers from two different cultural and language backgrounds. When one of your child's teachers speaks the home language of your family and has familiarity with the cultural patterns that you grew up with, that teacher can help tremendously with the social and emotional side of learning. Social and emotional factors strongly influence children's language acquisition and comfort with school. Until students feel safe and secure with their teachers and fellow students, it is hard for learning to take place. Having two teachers to negotiate the different cultural patterns in school and to provide a "bicultural comfort zone" for students makes all the difference. As classes become more like home and family, they become more heart-centered. That is our goal in the dual language program.

Teenagers are a serious concern for parents and schools, with all the dramatic changes that occur in their bodies and brains during this time. Until these youngsters mature into adulthood, they may be drawn into behaviors that are risky and dangerous, such as drug use and gang affiliation. Social and emotional support provided by the bilingual/bicultural teachers and counselors at school can make a critical difference in your children's lives. Equally important at this time is the relationship with family. Communication gaps between you and your teenager can occur when your child has experienced schooling only in English and is losing the family language. But if you have been able to continue to use your family home language for communications with your teenager, you can work in partnership with the dual language school to help your child mature and grow. You can transmit the values of your family heritage when you speak to your children in the language that you know best. That language best expresses your cultural insights, knowledge, wisdom, and adult perspective. Ideally, your children come to appreciate, respect, and value the richness of their cultural heritage. As they grow older they will also value the importance of bilingualism for maintaining intergenerational communication with their grandparents and other family members who speak the heritage language.

Expanding Thinking Skills

Our children are our future. We all want our kids to be smart. We want our children to know how to solve life's problems. Schools think about this and try to make classes relevant, but for students, the school curriculum can sometimes feel less connected to the world outside of school. As students reach middle school age and older, they see major differences between the adult world and what they are studying in school.

Bilinguals are smarter. How can dual language classes keep students excited and motivated to complete high school? When your children have the opportunity to learn to read and write and study other subjects in their home language, does that really help them do better in English? The answer from the research is a very strong YES (Collier & Thomas, 2009, 2014; Thomas & Collier, 2012, 2014). One of the most important reasons is that this helps your children develop more parts of their brains, expanding their thinking skills. We are all born with a human brain that has the ability to learn multiple languages. Monolingual humans use a smaller percentage of their brains' capabilities, but bilinguals develop and use more brain capacity. Bilinguals expand their abilities far beyond that of monolinguals. Proficient bilinguals are better at problem solving, creativity, mental flexibility, attention to detail, working memory, conflict management, task switching, and many other areas being studied in current research on bilinguals (see Figure 1.1). When children study in two languages, they expand their thinking skills. This will help them to be very competent adults.

First language and cognitive development. Another important reason to enroll your children in the dual language program is the relationship between continuous development of your children's first language and cognitive development (thinking skills). Children must develop thinking skills in their first language until age 12 to have normal cognitive development and to be successful in their second language. When children stop using their first language at a young age, their development of thinking skills is interrupted and slowed as they switch to their new language, and they may not do well in school. That switch to English causes a slowdown in understanding of grade-level content. By the end of elementary school, our research shows that students who do not continue to study school subjects in their home language are typically two to four grades behind students who attend dual language classes. The dual language classes help students stay on grade level while they are learning English. When they are meeting grade-level content standards in their native language, they are continuing cognitive development with no slowdown. That is very important for their long-term success as adults.

Figure 3.1

First Language Acquisition and Cognitive Development are Closely Related

- Cognitive development in first language until age 12 is the key to successful second language acquisition and curricular mastery.
- Interrupting a child's normal cognitive development by **changing from one monolingual instructional language to another** can result in:
    - cognitive development slowdowns (making students less cognitively capable),
    - lower achievement across the curriculum, and
    - reduced acquisition of second language (e.g., English).
- A child who reaches <u>full</u> cognitive development in first language <u>and</u> in second language enjoys cognitive advantages over monolinguals in either language.
- To reach optimum second language achievement, **emphasize consistent, uninterrupted cognitive and academic development in both languages.**

This prevents negative cognitive effects and keeps children on grade level in achievement for full acquisition of the second language.

Copyright © 1996-2017, W.P. Thomas and V.P. Collier. All rights reserved.

Parents' first language and cognitive development. Your role as parents is extremely important. You assist your children's cognitive development when you use your family language at home. You raised your children in that home language from their birth to the present. When you use your native language with your children, you help them develop cognitively every day of their life. All the natural activities that you do with your children at home stimulate the development of thinking skills. For example, when you use your family language as you do things together, such as shopping, cooking, cleaning, discussing family values, or sharing family traditions, you are helping your children to develop thinking skills. Your children need to continue nonstop cognitive development in their home language both at home and at school. In a dual language program, the school will add the second language at no cost to the children's first language and cognitive development.

Raising bilinguals from birth. Some parents are already bilingual and have chosen to raise their children bilingually from birth on. This works very well, too. In fact, this is quite common in many regions of the world. When you raise your children bilingually, they are constantly developing cognitively in both languages. When bilingual children reach school age, it is a great advantage for them to be schooled bilingually. Your children need to continue using the two languages, including literacy development in both of those languages at school (when the language is written). Dual language programs continue nonstop cognitive development in both of your family's languages. As your children move through the school grades, they will continue to develop the proficiency in both languages needed for each grade level. Proficient bilinguals outscore monolinguals on all types of tests, including measures of creative intelligence (Baker, 2011; Collier & Thomas, 2017). Your children will be better prepared for all the challenges of adult life.

Parents and Dual Language Schools in the U.S.

An increasing number of U.S. schools want your family and your children to be bilingual or multilingual. In the recent past, many bilingual parents have been discouraged by the attitudes of some monolingual educators who do not appreciate the importance of bilingualism. Your parents or grandparents may have been punished for using their home language at school. But the world is changing rapidly, and attitudes are changing, too. Dual language schools are becoming more and more in demand in the U.S. as people realize their value.

As these schools develop, they need more bilingual teachers. Graduates of dual language programs can be strong candidates for positions as teachers and administrators. This is one example of many professional fields that increasingly require bilinguals in the workforce. Your children have an exciting future ahead of them when they develop their bilingualism to full proficiency in school, because this will greatly expand their employment possibilities.

Those of you who are Spanish speakers know that Spanish is a major world language—the second most spoken language after Mandarin Chinese. There are now more native speakers of Spanish throughout the world than there are native speakers of English (*Ethnologue*, 2017, *www.ethnologue.com/statistics/size*). In the past, Spanish and many other world languages were spoken by immigrants all over the U.S. It was in the 19th and 20th centuries, as our country was establishing its cultural and linguistic identity, that English came into prominence as the dominant language of the U.S. As a result, both discrimination and prejudice were expressed towards those who spoke languages other than English. This pattern is changing now, and Spanish and other world languages are currently popular choices of native-English-speaking parents for their children attending dual language programs. U.S. history surrounding the Spanish language still influences some attitudes towards Spanish, so it is important for Spanish-speaking parents to remember that Spanish is a "power language" just like English, and your children will benefit enormously by becoming Spanish-English bilinguals, able to communicate in two major world languages (Collier & Thomas, 2013).

Parent leadership and advocacy. In the U.S., school leaders expect parents to actively participate in schools. This is not customary in all cultures, so at first, it can be difficult for immigrant parents to understand this responsibility. What kind of parent participation is expected in a dual language program? Initially, you will be encouraged to attend parent meetings at school. Sometimes meetings are held with your children's teachers to discuss your children's progress. Since dual language teachers are bilingual, parents who are not yet proficient in English should feel comfortable talking to the teacher and welcome to discuss any concerns or suggestions.

Dual language schools often provide a rich variety of parent programs during after-school hours, offering community services that families may need. These can include exchanges of skills among parents, workshops on topics requested by parents and teachers, and language classes for the parents. The most meaningful meetings are usually organized by the parents, to serve the parents' needs. For example, new immigrant groups might sponsor regular meetings to inform each other about housing opportunities, relations with law enforcement agencies, schooling in the U.S., adult education classes, and other possibilities.

For dual language schools, parent advocacy is extremely important. Once you understand how dual language classes function and the reasons they work so well, the school can use your support in explaining these things to other families who are considering enrolling their children in the program. This is a program of choice. Often new immigrants are initially unsure about placing their children in the dual language classes, because they are anxious for their children to learn English as quickly as possible. But the research is clear that this is the best program for students to learn English while keeping up with grade-level schoolwork through the home language. You can help these parents understand why keeping up in school and learning English are so important for their children. You can use the information in this chapter, along with your own experiences, to make your case.

Figure 3.2

Dual Language Students ...

- score higher on achievement tests in both their first and second languages,
- are more engaged with classroom instruction,
- have stronger bicultural identity and self-esteem,
- are significantly more mature for their age,
- are happier and more motivated,
- achieve higher high school graduation rates,
- receive more scholarships to study at universities, and
- are successful bilingual professionals as adults.

Copyright © 2017, W.P. Thomas and V.P. Collier. All rights reserved.

Conclusion

The research clearly shows that all groups of students do well in dual language education—Latinos, Asians, Caucasians, African Americans, American Indians, English learners, native English speakers, students in poverty, students of middle- or upper-class background, students with special education needs—everyone benefits. Through the hard work and commitment of the school community, students, and participating families, well-implemented dual language programs can produce remarkable results. Dual language students score higher on tests in both English and the other program language. Their attendance is better; they have fewer disciplinary referrals; and they are more engaged in lessons. They are cognitively more mature for their age; they are more motivated; they have more confidence and higher self-esteem; and they are happier. They have more cross-cultural awareness, higher graduation rates, more scholarships to study at universities, and higher-paying jobs because they are proficient bilinguals.

Chapter Four
Understanding Second Language Acquisition in Dual Language Classes

Dual language classes are quite different from traditional language classes! Dual language students develop their second language by using it with their classmates as they study mathematics, science, social studies, language arts, music, art, and physical education. With the support of carefully planned instruction, the English learners and native English speakers acquire each other's languages through a process that is very *similar to the natural acquisition of their first language*. This is the best way to learn a language. The natural, subconscious, developmental process of language acquisition is always a complex and amazing feat!

In a traditional language class, the focus is on learning *about* the language—the grammar, spelling, vocabulary, and how you put sentences together. In contrast, while a dual language teacher includes language objectives in each lesson, the main focus is the subject matter, such as a science experiment or math problem solving. The language objectives remind the teacher to support the students' ability to talk, read, and write about what they're learning. Dual language teachers teach all of the curricular objectives for their grade level. They make the lessons accessible to the second language learners in their class by providing additional clues for understanding the lesson and opportunities for meaningful language use. Their language arts classes in each language reinforce the second language acquired through content areas with explanations, study, and practice in how the language works—and by helping students acquire and practice reading and writing skills in their first and second languages. But overall, in dual language classes much of the language learning that students go through is in support of the content learning through activities in the school curriculum. This is natural language acquisition, just as very young children acquired their first language (Krashen, 1981). It is a powerful way to learn a new language—much more effective than language lessons in isolation.

First Language Acquisition

Birth to age 5. So how do we pick up our first language? Is it quick and easy? Not really ... it is a complex, lifelong process. First language acquisition starts at birth, or possibly even in the womb. For young children, development of oral language is universal. Given no physical disabilities and no social isolation from humans, all children of the world innately develop a full and complex oral language system. A 5-year-old child just beginning school has already subconsciously picked up listening and speaking skills in the family language in pronunciation, vocabulary, grammar, semantics (meaning), and pragmatics (social context), at the cognitive level of a 5-year-old. This is an incredible accomplishment. Parents often think of this child as fully proficient, but the most gifted 5-year-old is not yet halfway through the process of first language development.

Home dialects. Sometimes school personnel who are not trained in language acquisition might talk about a kindergartener having "no language" or "limited language." What they really mean is that the child is not familiar with the standard variety used in school. Linguists analyzing American English dialects in depth have found that each language system used in a given community has a full grammar and vocabulary system equally as complex as the standard variety—just different. Well-trained dual language teachers understand that their students' home dialects are to be respected and valued. Dual language teachers then assist with the process of bidialectal acquisition of the standard varieties of the two languages of school (Wolfram & Christian, 1989).

School years. Natural first language acquisition continues both in school and at home for children ages 6 to 12. Through informal and formal language use, they acquire subtle phonological distinctions, vocabulary and semantic development, grammar rules, formal thought patterns, and complex aspects of pragmatics (social contexts of language use) in the oral system of their first language. Reading and writing taught in language arts classes include all the dimensions of language listed above, becoming cognitively more and more complex with each grade level and for each subject in school. A student entering post-secondary classes still faces enormous amounts of new vocabulary to acquire in each discipline of study, as well as continuing acquisition of reading and writing skills.

Adults. By young adulthood, first language proficiency development is nothing short of a phenomenon, and yet we continue to increase our knowledge and uses of our native language throughout our lifetime. Even as adults, we are always learning new vocabulary, picking up new aspects of social and workplace language, and expanding our writing skills. Language use is constantly changing, and we subconsciously absorb these new language patterns into our own oral and written communications with others. The newest communication technologies dramatically reinforce this constant change process in language use. Children and young adults help us keep up with these new ways to use language and are often speedier than adults with new technologies. Language acquisition is an unending process—it continues throughout our life (Collier, 1995; Collier & Thomas, 2009, Figure 4.1, p. 33).

Second Language Acquisition

Natural developmental processes. From the first days of exposure to a second language, whatever our age, we use some of the same innate processes that we used to acquire our first language. We go through developmental stages similar to those in first language acquisition, making some of the same types of errors in grammatical markers that young children make, picking up chunks of language without knowing precisely what each word means, and relying on others who speak that language to provide modified speech that we can at least partially comprehend.

The evidence for an innate process in second language acquisition comes from research on the types of errors that students make as they go through increasing exposure to the second language. At first, researchers assumed that students' errors were mostly structures transferred from their first language. Now there is substantial research evidence that many error patterns are predictable across all learners, regardless of their first language or the formal instruction given to them in the second language (Ellis, 1994).

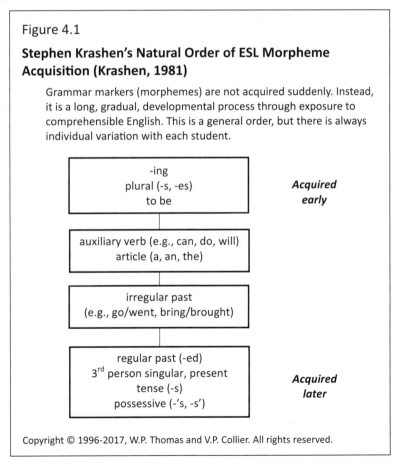

Stages of acquisition. ESL learners pass through a predictable sequence of stages while acquiring English negation, interrogation, and relative clauses, whatever their first language. In the first stage, most English learners develop a word order that is different from standard English word order, and they omit some sentence constituents. In the second stage, the learners begin to use more standard English word order and most required sentence constituents are present (subject-verb), but grammatical accuracy is still missing. The third stage leads to more systematic and meaningful usage of grammar markers (although still with plenty of errors). In the fourth stage, the English learner increasingly uses more complex sentence structures. This all happens gradually with increasing exposure to the language. The rate at which learners reach each stage varies with each individual student. Likewise, the sequence of acquisition of specific structures of English varies from student to student. But understanding that ESL students pass through general developmental stages common across all second language learners can help teachers and parents to have patience with the process.

A nonlinear process. It also helps to know that the process is not linear. Language acquisition is more like a zig-zag process. One day you can feel immensely satisfied that a student seems to have mastered a particular grammar marker, but the next day in another context, the error shows up again. This is to be expected. Perhaps the teacher is focusing on regular past tense in English (the morpheme "-ed" in its written form, pronounced three different ways). Students have reached the stage where they are actually starting to get the morpheme correct some of the time. If you follow one student's pattern of errors in regular past tense across a variety of natural activities in use of oral and written English, you will see that it is an "up and down" process with mastery not demonstrated consistently once it has been taught or picked up. Instead, the student gradually begins to get the morpheme right in more and more contexts until finally the subtleties of the use of that particular structure (e.g., exceptions, spelling variations, pronunciation contexts) have become a subconscious part of the learner's language system. But this takes time, and formal teaching does not speed up the natural developmental process. At the same time, teachers serve the important role of providing consistent and appropriate support with targeted instruction and ample opportunities to use the language to facilitate the natural process.

> **Figure 4.2**
>
> **Pattern of Acquisition of Grammar Structures in Second Language**
>
>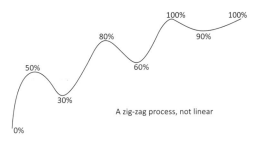
>
> A zig-zag process, not linear
>
> Percentage of times student produces correct form as proficiency in second language increases.
>
> Second language acquisition is a natural, gradual, long-term developmental process.
>
> For the early stages of second language acquisition, it is …
> - Less important to focus on error correction
> - More important to focus on communication and content
> - Less important to focus on acquisition of discrete points of language
> - More important to focus on:
>   - thinking in the language
>   - extensive development of vocabulary in context
>   - integrated listening, speaking, reading, writing across the curriculum
>
> Copyright © 1996-2017, W.P. Thomas and V.P. Collier. All rights reserved

Let's take another example: acquisition of the third person singular present tense in English, which is the "-s" added to verbs. ESL textbooks typically introduce this morpheme in beginning lessons. It is easy to teach because there are few exceptions to the rules for its use. Students may get it right on a written test when they have plenty of time to think about the rule. But most first- and second-year ESL students will continue to leave off the "-s" when they are speaking or writing English at normal speed. This morpheme does not become a part of the subconscious, acquired system until after several years of exposure to standard English. Many regional varieties of English omit this morpheme in spoken English, so students may hear it less in natural conversational usage. It doesn't hurt to teach the "-s" early, but teachers should not expect students to demonstrate mastery until they have reached the developmental stage when they are ready to pick up its appropriate usage. Acquisition of any given structure of English does not occur simply by formally teaching that structure, but through exposure to correct use of the structure over time in many different linguistic contexts that are meaningful to the student (Krashen, 1981).

Therefore, **basic skills approaches do not work well for second language acquisition.** Lockstep, sequenced curricular materials and tests that insist on mastery of each discrete point in language before moving on to the next are a disaster for second language acquisition. The natural order of second language acquisition is a much stronger force than any textbook writer's view of simple to complex and other attempts at "logical" sequencing of language points to be mastered. Basic skills approaches do not work because they are often based on some author's view of the order in which each discrete point in language should be learned. Basic skills approaches also use discrete-point language tests as a gatekeeper for access to more meaningful schoolwork. When basic skills are emphasized at low cognitive levels, students are not allowed to do cognitively complex work appropriate to their age level, and their natural language and cognitive development is slowed (Hudelson, 1994).

Why should this matter to policy makers and families? Policy makers are watching the school district's test scores to meet state accountability standards. Families want to see their children do well on the tests and make good grades. The basic skills tests hold children back by not measuring meaningful, cognitively complex language development. District-level policy makers need to work closely with the dual language staff to choose cognitively and academically appropriate curricular materials and tests that truly measure students' levels of achievement across all subjects of the curriculum. Additionally, the content and results of the curricular tests must be provided and equally valued in both languages.

Focus on language use. Well-trained dual language teachers recognize that second language acquisition is a dynamic, creative, innate process, best developed through contextual, meaningful activities that focus on students' language use—combined with guidance from the teacher that sometimes involves a focus on language form. The teacher is a facilitator of the process. In the early acquisition stages, errors need not be viewed as lack of mastery but as positive steps in the process. The focus for dual language students just beginning development of their second language should be on language use, not on language form. Correct form will come with time and further use of the language.

The ideal context for language learning. Dual language classes provide a natural context for second language acquisition through positive interaction with peers of the same age. Language develops through using the language collaboratively with friends. The classroom materials must be authentic, interesting, meaningful, and relevant to the world the students know outside of school—and one step beyond the students' present levels. The dual language classroom provides a social setting in which the two language groups can learn how to work together for each other's benefit. This results in natural first and second language acquisition while keeping up with all of their curricular subjects with each year of school.

How Long Does It Take to Develop Second Language Proficiency?

The answer to the question of how long it takes is, "It depends." Many, many factors influence how efficiently second language can be acquired—including, for example, how well you have developed your first language, your age, how you are going to use the second language, the amount of schooling you have had, and the social-emotional context in which you're learning the new language. In this book, we are focusing on the school context for learning and using the new language. At school, students use their languages in social contexts as they're moving from class to class and for lunch and recess, as well as within their homeroom. We refer to this as social language. During class time, more of the focus is on academic uses of the languages. Each school subject has its own way of expressing language and we refer to this as academic language. Let's examine how long it takes to acquire each of these aspects of school language.

Social language: 2–5 years. Sometimes you might hear a school staff member referring to an ESL student with the comment, "She speaks perfectly good English." This comment implies fluency, but conversational language is only one small portion of the language skills needed to be successful in school. When we use the term "social language," we mean informal oral and written language used to interact meaningfully with others in everyday activities. Conversational language provides extra help to the second language learner by providing contextual clues to meaning, including nonverbal cues, estimated to be as much as 70% of the total communication process. Social language can also include basic literacy for use in shopping, transportation, health services, or sending email and text messages. Cummins (1979) first introduced the term "Basic Interpersonal Communicative Skills (BICS)" to refer to social language.

Linguists estimate that getting a "working command" of the social aspects of a new language takes children anywhere from 2 to 5 years. In order for social (and academic) language to be acquired in the dual language classroom, certain components are critical: (1) the learners must realize they need to learn the new language and be motivated to do so; (2) the native speakers of the new language need to know it well enough to interact meaningfully with the learners; and (3) the class activities must be designed to facilitate the two language groups interacting collaboratively with each other as they master the curriculum together (Wong Fillmore, 1991).

Academic language: 6–9 years. The context for academic language development is school, and this will also eventually include language use in professional work settings. In school, each subject has its own unique vocabulary, grammar, and discourse (formal thought) patterns of academic language. Academic uses of language become more demanding with each succeeding grade level, through increasingly abstract written language and fewer and fewer contextual clues to meaning. Cummins (1979) added cognition in his definition of school language with his term "Cognitive Academic Language Proficiency (CALP)." We will discuss cognitive development and its important connections to academic language in the last section of this chapter.

Academic language is an extension of social language, and together they define a continuum. A well-trained dual language teacher includes social and academic language development in every lesson. A lesson might start with social language through activities that stimulate students' own knowledge and experience connected to the lesson. Contextual support then comes through peer interaction in cooperative learning structures and use of pantomiming, storytelling, puppets, visuals, maps, charts, manipulatives, the media, technology, music, art, chants, movement, and many more possibilities. New knowledge is developed and applied through interactive tasks that stimulate students' cognitive and academic growth, as the curricular material moves from hands-on to more complex, abstract thinking, with support for both oral and written activities.

When we define academic language proficiency as grade-level achievement in all the subjects of the school curriculum, it takes an average of 6 years for students to reach this level in their second language. *Dual language students reach grade level in a second language faster than students in any other program.* In particular, two-way dual language students achieve this faster than one-way dual language students. In two-way classes, peers who speak the second language are present, and they accelerate second language development through peer interaction as they work together on the curricular material. One-way classes have fewer peers who speak the second language. For this reason, we recommend that one-way programs continue through the middle school years in order for students to reach grade-level performance standards. Students who have been in one-way dual language classes since kindergarten can completely close the gap in their second language by eighth grade.

How about other programs for English learners, such as ESL-only or transitional bilingual education taught for only 2 to 3 years? Sadly, none of them completely close the gap for the students to reach grade-level achievement. For English learners, all-English instruction in the mainstream leads to the lowest long-term achievement and the highest dropout rate. The main influence on success in second language is how much schooling students have had in their first language. In other words, more years of school in first language equals success in second language. This is one reason why high-quality dual language classes are superior to all other programs. Dual language students receive instruction through both languages for the number of years needed to reach grade-level achievement. With more years of dual language schooling (K–8 and PK–12), English learners can reach achievement above grade level.

How about native English speakers attending dual language classes? If they stay in the program throughout Grades K–5, they will also typically reach grade-level achievement in their second language after 6 years of schooling through the two languages. In English, they will be scoring above grade level. Bilingually schooled students typically outperform monolingually schooled students in the long term. We encourage these students to continue into the middle and high school years as well. That prepares them to use their bilingualism and biliteracy as adults in their professional fields (Collier & Thomas, 2009, 2017; Thomas & Collier, 2012).

Role of First Language

Academic language development in a second language is directly connected to first language schooling. This powerful variable has more impact on second language acquisition for school than any other influence. Academic skills, literacy development, concept formation, and subject knowledge developed in the first language will all transfer to a second language. In dual language classes, the transfer also occurs from second language to first language.

Subject knowledge. In a study that we conducted examining ESL students' mathematics achievement, 700 adolescent Asian immigrants outperformed native English speakers on a standardized mathematics test administered in English, after only 2 years of acquisition of English in the U.S. These students had received higher levels of mathematics instruction in their home countries before emigrating to the U.S., far ahead of that required in the U.S. curriculum for their grade level. Once they built enough of a base in English mathematics vocabulary, they were able to demonstrate their high level of mathematics knowledge, even though they had not taken these courses in English (Collier & Thomas, 1989).

Dual language high school students demonstrate this concept of transfer of complex material from first to second language and also the reverse. Approximately half of their courses are taught in the non-English language and half in English. A dual language student might take one of the core science courses required for graduation in English. The next year the sequential required science course is offered in the non-English language. New vocabulary and concept development is always a part of each course, so the switch from one language to the other is reinforced by review covered at the beginning of the semester and throughout the course. The students' deep academic proficiency in both languages supports their work, so that they do not need to repeat any courses in the other language. Subject knowledge is there and can be demonstrated on a test in either language.

Literacy development. Reading and writing are essential skills for all schoolwork. How does literacy transfer to second language? For English learners, skills developed in first language literacy are not only easily transferred but are also crucial to academic success in the second language (Beeman & Urow, 2013; Escamilla et al., 2014). In our longitudinal studies, English learners with less than 3 to 4 years of first language schooling are typically 2 to 3 years behind their first language-schooled ESL peers in academic achievement in English. Those who have never learned to read their first language may be three or more grade levels below the achievement of immigrants who arrive in the U.S. on grade level in their native language (Collier & Thomas, 2017).

It is a common-sense assumption that literacy transfer can work for languages that have similar writing systems, but how about non-Roman-alphabet languages such as Arabic, Hindi, Mandarin Chinese, Hebrew, or Korean? Some of these written scripts have right-left or vertical directionality and very different ways of writing phonemes or word symbols when paired with English in a dual language program. Even so, researchers have found that more than half of the skills acquired in the process of learning to read are universal skills, regardless of the written language system (Thonis, 1994). For example, once a student has picked up the significance of following a consistent pattern in directionality, that student has mastered at least half of the skill. Very quickly, a reader of right-left script catches on that English goes left-right and then top to bottom. Having acquired directionality in the first language, the student is looking for the pattern of directionality in the second language. Many universal reading strategies can be applied across all the world's languages. Dual language teachers often say that when they formally introduce reading in the second language, they do not need to re-teach many aspects of reading. The students already know how to read, and with carefully planned instructional support, they have independently applied their reading skills to their other language.

Special Messages to Parents on More Language Issues

To English-speaking parents in 90:10 programs. One of the big challenges for dual language staff is how to explain to English-speaking parents how 90:10 works. We can assure you that based on research, 90:10 is the most effective model. If your school district has chosen the 90:10 model, that means that *all* the students will learn to read in the non-English language first. This works, but it is a contradiction with the paragraphs you just read about English learners and the importance of developing literacy in their first language. How does this work for English-speaking students who learn to read in their new language before they learn to read in English?

Your children are contextually advantaged because they are speakers of English—the dominant or majority language of the U.S. Outside of school, English is used in their neighborhood, in their uses of media and technology, in the stores, and at home. They know that their native language is valued and important. In addition, your children are secure in their identity. They are what linguists call "additive bilinguals." They are adding a second language at no cost to their first language. They will continue to develop cognitively in English, even though the school will emphasize the use of English less (only 10% of the time) during the first 2 years of their schooling. Your children get large amounts of support for cognitive development in English in the world outside of school and at home. In the 90:10 dual language classes, it often happens that the English speakers immediately start applying their knowledge of reading skills in their second language to English literacy development. By second grade when English literacy is formally introduced, the English-speaking students have already picked up reading in English on their own and they quickly attain grade-level skills in English literacy development.

How 90:10 works for both student groups. The 90:10 dual language model emphasizes the non-English language first (90% of the time) to give a jump start to both groups of students. The native English speakers can use this intensive development of their second language when the curriculum is very hands-on. Since they are only exposed to the second language during the school day, this will advance their proficiency development so that when they get to fourth and fifth grade, they won't hold the class back for lack of ability in the non-English language. On the other hand, the English learners need a jump-start in their first language to start school on grade level and stay there. They are speakers of a minority language in the U.S. They are enrolled in dual language classes to become additive bilinguals just like the native English speakers. But because their native language is not supported by the broader society, they need extra support in their first language. They also need to know that their first language is just as important as English.

Nonstop cognitive development in first language. The key to understanding the role of first language in the academic development of second language is to understand the function of uninterrupted cognitive development. Earlier in Chapter 3, we explained this relationship briefly. But this is such an important concept that we will go into more detail here about the intertwining of first language and cognition. This is an important key to why dual language classes work so well for so many different types of students.

Dual language curricula increase the cognitive complexity of schoolwork, while the cross-cultural knowledge building that students experience leads to higher student engagement. Students pay more attention when there are many exciting things going on that they are able to understand. It's more stimulating to learn about different ways of living life, new ways to solve problems, new perceptions of what life is all about. *These two outcomes are of the greatest significance for dual language students: increased cognitive development and greater student engagement with learning.*

Parents' role in cognitive development. How does the increased cognitive development in dual language classes connect to your children's first language? Cognitive development starts at birth. So does first language. As spoken language emerges, the child can express what s/he is thinking. As a parent, you stimulate your child's cognitive and linguistic development by using the language(s) that you know best. The family language is the one in which you are cognitively mature. You constantly stimulate your children's first language and cognitive development when you ask questions, make decisions together, discuss daily activities, give moral support, set goals together, and share family values. Sharing household responsibilities with your children also continues cognitive development—shopping, cooking, cleaning, and talking about everything you do together. All family activities—such as telling stories, sharing family heritage, music, art, games, sports, reading books, going places, celebrating special occasions—with shared talking in the family language are stimuli for developing the brain, getting those neurons active. It is very important that this cognitive development through first language (or languages, if you are raising your children bilingually) continue throughout their childhood. It is not necessary for you to switch to another language that you do not know well when you are interacting with your children at home. In fact, you should use your strongest language with your children, since you present yourself as a cognitively mature adult in this way. Your children need your nonstop support and modeling for cognitive development through the language that you know best. Keeping your home language and using it often is the best contribution to support the school's work with your children (Collier & Thomas, 2009, Figure 4.3, p. 36).

Cognitive threshold in first language: Age 12. Children need to reach a cognitive threshold in their first language in order to avoid negative cognitive effects. If your children can continue to develop their first language until at least age 12, their cognitive development will be adequately supported, and they will build on this development throughout life. We have learned from the research on bilinguals that immigrants who have been forced to lose their first language at a young age do less well in school because their cognitive development has been limited. Linguists call this "subtractive bilingualism," when the second language replaces the first language before cognitive maturity has been reached around age 12. Dual language classes produce "additive bilinguals." Both groups of students, the native English speakers and the English learners, are able to continue nonstop cognitive development, because they are studying their subjects through both languages. They are adding a new language without stopping the development of their first language.

English learners who do not receive dual language schooling through both their home language and English are sometimes inappropriately referred to special education support or placed on a slower track. As subtractive bilinguals, their cognitive slowdown when taught all in English does not seem evident in the early grades, but as the curriculum gets cognitively more complex with each succeeding grade, they are not able to keep up with their classmates. On the other hand, English learners who receive schooling through both languages and whose parents continue using their family language at home become additive bilinguals, proficient in two languages, cognitively mature in both, and prepared for their adult lives as bilingual professionals (Collier & Thomas, 2009).

Age Differences in Second Language Acquisition

What is the "ideal age" to begin a second language? As we explained earlier in this chapter, there is no easy answer. Your age can make a difference when you first begin learning a second language. But to understand how age affects the acquisition process, you need to consider many other variables that interact with age. Age does not operate in isolation as a cause agent. Students of all ages can be very effective learners of language. At the same time, each age group can experience different interacting factors that influence the acquisition process. Let's take a look at general patterns in age differences.

Infants and toddlers: Simultaneous bilinguals. Young children who are raised from birth with exposure to two languages experience a process similar to first language acquisition. Using their innate language capacity, most children go through an initial stage of combining the two languages into one system. As they move through succeeding stages, assuming that they receive approximately equal exposure to the two languages, they gradually learn to separate the two languages into two distinct systems by around age 5 or 6.

For young bilinguals, language mixing during the preschool years is quite common as a natural stage in the developmental process of language acquisition. It is a big mistake to diagnose language mixing as a learning disability for this age group. As long as a young child receives regular exposure to both languages over time and experiences continuing cognitive development in both languages, s/he will reach the same level of proficiency in two languages as that of a child acquiring one language. Furthermore, children who are fortunate enough in school to be able to continue building academic proficiency in both languages through the dual language program will experience cognitive advantages over monolinguals.

Parents often wonder if they should separate the two languages, with, for example, one parent speaking only Spanish and the other speaking only English. This used to be the advice given to parents several decades ago. But we now have considerable research evidence that separating the two languages is not necessary, as long as the child gets equal exposure to and practice with both languages (Baker, 2011). By around school age, the child will eventually sort out the two language systems as part of the natural, subconscious process.

Preschoolers: Sequential bilinguals. Children who begin a second language sometime during the preschool years can be equally successful second language learners. However, one major interacting factor is crucial—continuing cognitive development in first language. Often well-meaning educators feel that preschoolers can get a head start on acquiring English by immersing the children in English at the expense of their first language. At this stage of their schooling, they usually appear to be doing very well since the curriculum has not yet become demanding. But those children whose cognitive development in first language was stopped or slowed in the preschool years tend to perform poorly on school measures across the curriculum as they move into the upper elementary grades. They never reached the "threshold" discussed in the previous section.

Children of low socioeconomic background or those whose parents have not had the opportunity to receive formal schooling are those most in danger of lost years of cognitive development due to an early switch to the second language in preschool. These children are better prepared academically when they attend preschool that is taught exclusively in their home language. In other words, at this age, cognitive development is much more important than the introduction of a second language. For these children, exposure to second language should be postponed until a solid cognitive and academic base is built in first language.

Ages 5–11. Continuing cognitive and academic development in the first language is also a crucial issue for children in elementary school. Success in a second language is more likely if literacy and thinking skills are fully developed in the first language through at least fifth grade. This age group is a great time to begin a second language. In fact, any age from birth to age 12 is a good time as long as cognitive and academic development in the first language is not stopped or slowed as the second language is introduced.

The big advantage children from birth to puberty have over older learners is pronunciation. The younger you are when you begin a second language, the less likely it is that you will retain or even develop an accent. Native-like pronunciation is not really a proficiency issue, assuming that you can be well understood with your accent. However, an accent can often change the social perceptions that native speakers have, such as assuming that your accent reflects limited proficiency in the languages. This can be quite frustrating and sometimes results in discriminatory treatment. Pronunciation is a concern for adolescents, young adults, and older adults, to be discussed next.

Adolescents and young adults. Research syntheses on the optimal age for beginning a second language have concluded that older students are more efficient learners, reaching proficiency levels in more cognitively complex uses of the second language faster than younger students (Collier, 1987). Adolescents and young adults have many advantages over the younger child *if they have received formal schooling in their first language.* Young adults' academic knowledge and experience with first language schooling assist them in second language schooling. Except for pronunciation, students of this age group are the most efficient learners of a second language because they are cognitively mature.

The main reason that we are fooled by young children's ability in second language is that the type of language a 5-year-old speaks is much less cognitively complex than that of a young adult. We are also often jealous of the native-like pronunciation that young children acquire quickly and their seeming ease in social interaction with speakers of the second language. But the process young children go through is just as complex as the experience of older learners, and it takes more time for young children to reach full academic proficiency in second language than for high school and university students, who have reached cognitive maturity and can transfer the academic knowledge base acquired in their first language to the second language.

Newly arriving immigrants of middle and high school age can benefit greatly from dual language classes. During the English instructional time, they will be working with content ESL teachers who can facilitate their development of the English language through the academic subjects. Courses taken in their native language help them advance academically while they are learning English. For older students who have received little or no formal schooling before they arrive, it is even more urgent that they receive courses through their first language because this will enable them to catch up faster.

Adults. Adult learners of a second language who are beyond their 20s when first introduced to the new language may have more difficulty than the adolescent or young adult. We have already discussed the issue of pronunciation, which is a concern for adults as well as adolescents and young adults. But older adults are quite capable of developing full proficiency in the second language with time, except for the likelihood of retaining an accent in pronunciation. At the same time, there are "maturational constraints" that can influence the process for adults, such as social access to speakers of the second language and a tendency to experience less cognitive flexibility as we get older. Adults also tend to be more inhibited learners than younger students. Older adults have been quite successful with third and fourth language acquisition if they are already proficient in their first two languages (Collier, 1987, 1988).

Summary. Overall, stating that one age is better than another to begin second language acquisition is misleading. This greatly oversimplifies the complex linguistic, sociocultural, cognitive, and academic factors that interact with age in the development of second language. However, beginning to acquire a second language in a dual language program that starts at preschool or kindergarten is a very good option that yields positive results by the end of the school years. In the next chapter, we continue a discussion of these factors by examining the social, emotional, and cultural influences on schooling through two languages.

Chapter Five
The Social, Emotional, and Cultural Heart of Dual Language Schooling

Another aspect of dual language classes that is so powerful for changing many students' school experiences into positive outcomes involves the social and emotional benefits that dual language students receive—far beyond the limits of traditional classes. Several factors help make this happen. The teachers bring a wealth of cultural experiences from their own diverse backgrounds into the mix of classroom activities as they reflect on the curricular objectives and think of ways to extend the lessons to reflect bicultural and multicultural perspectives. The students themselves add to this diversity (social class and ethnicity) as they work in bilingual pairs and small groups. Their work together expands each other's perspectives on life and guides them to creative solutions to the curricular problems presented to them. The emotional support builds among students and teachers as they create a safe, loving atmosphere within their classrooms. This is the heart of learning, and when this comfort zone is reached, accelerated learning takes place (Collier & Thomas, 2009, Chapter 4).

Social and Cultural Processes

Researchers in the natural development of language consider the social and cultural aspects to be equally important to linguistic and cognitive processes. At school, social processes influence the development of language and learning in powerful ways. Teachers address the emotional side of learning by setting up a classroom context where students can work together in cooperative tasks rather than competing with each other. Teachers who truly understand the sociocultural context in which learning can take place know that there are many societal influences outside of school that can affect students' response to learning, in both positive and negative ways. Examples include students' perceptions of each other from interethnic relations within the community, cultural stereotyping, intergroup relations, equal or different status of the groups represented in the school, social and psychological distance between speakers of the two languages of their classroom, and neighborhood patterns of assimilation (subtractive, losing heritage culture) or acculturation (additive, affirming multiple cultures) (Collier, 1995). Young children emotionally receive clues that these kinds of patterns are present, but they rarely understand the social history that led to these challenges. Older students, however, are frequently very much aware and resentful of the social complexities of the world that adults have passed on to them (California Department of Education, 1986).

> Figure 5.1
> **Examples of Social and Cultural Processes in Second Language Acquisition**
>
> At school:
> - Language use at school (equal affirmation of students' first and second languages)
> - A cooperative classroom learning environment
> - Intergroup cooperation/hostility within school
>
> Student's past and present life experiences:
> - Student's socioeconomic status
> - Student's past formal schooling
> - Escape from war or other conflicts
>
> Affective factors:
> - High/low anxiety
> - Self-confidence/self-esteem
>
> Societal factors:
> - Social and psychological distance between language groups
> - Perceptions of each group in interethnic relations
> - Cultural stereotyping
> - Intergroup hostility
> - Cultural and community attitudes toward schooling
> - Subordinate status of a minority group
> - Patterns of assimilation (losing first culture when acquiring second culture) or acculturation (acquiring and affirming both cultures)
>
> Copyright © 1996-2017, W.P. Thomas and V.P. Collier. All rights reserved.

In dual language classes. Bilingual teachers cannot ignore these issues and must address them carefully. Caring and conscientious teachers who are cross-culturally aware can create a classroom context with the power to overcome potential social blocks to learning. The advantage of team teaching in the dual language program brings two professional heads together to resolve many of these concerns. Bilingual counselors added to the staff can enhance the responses to social issues that emerge within the school context.

In dual language schools. Schools reflect the community and the broader society, but they do not have to be limited by existing societal patterns. Dual language schools can be institutions of change—places where teachers, students, and staff of many varied backgrounds join together to transform tensions between groups and create a new neighborhood context for the benefit of all. A two-way dual language school joins together language-majority and language-minority families, creating cross-cultural curricular experiences taught through two languages with the goal of additive bilingualism for all students. With equal status given to the two languages and a multicultural curriculum, social and emotional support is provided for all, leading to students' confidence in self-identity and high cognitive development (García, Skutnabb-Kangas, Torres-Guzmán, 2006).

In the sections that follow, as we visit several examples of social and cultural processes at work, keep in mind that these are only glimpses of the wide range of life experiences that can influence students' different responses to learning opportunities. These examples remind us that students and families may face complex issues that powerfully impact the learning process in second language and academic achievement. Extensive research from anthropology, sociology, sociolinguistics, psychology, and education informs this aspect of the learning process.

Examples of Social and Cultural Processes Affecting Education

Recently arriving immigrants to the U.S. come from all over the world. In fact, the rate of global mobility is at an all-time high because of major political, economic, or environmental upheavals that disrupt lives and because of instant worldwide communications that inform potential immigrants of better conditions elsewhere. Many nations are currently experiencing dramatic increases in immigration, and the U.S. is no exception.

Immigrants are typically seeking refuge from conditions of war, from severe economic disruption, or from political oppression in their home countries. Some are even unaccompanied children who, at great risk to themselves, are seeking family members already in the U.S. Often, they have experienced interrupted or limited schooling in their home countries prior to leaving, typically for reasons of war or political instability. They may have experienced personally devastating events, such as brutality and violence, life in refugee camps, and/or the loss of family members; they may be suffering from trauma experienced during critical developmental stages. Thus, they may be angry, anxious, scared, withdrawn, or severely depressed. By their mere presence here, they demonstrate that they are survivors—risk-takers with great human potential. If these students are to realize their dreams of a better life in their new country, we educators must address their very special social, academic, and emotional needs (Coelho, 1994; Stewart, 1993).

These students especially need extensive first language academic support to develop literacy, mathematics, science, and social studies knowledge as quickly as possible to make up missed years of academic instruction. They also need abundant emotional support and counseling to deal with the scars of violence they may have witnessed and the continuing trauma of establishing stable family relations in their new country and meeting their basic survival needs.

Escape from war: Southeast Asian refugees. An interesting study examined 6,750 Southeast Asian boat people who emigrated to the U.S. following devastating hardships suffered in war and relocation camps. The researchers found that the strongest predictors of these students' academic success in U.S. schools were parents' maintenance of first language at home, both oral and written, as well as a strong retention of cultural traditions and values, including a supportive home environment that values education. In the past, the families in the study had not received extensive opportunities for formal schooling in their home countries—education was a privilege reserved mainly for the upper classes. Yet in spite of parents' lack of formal education, they were able to provide the family support needed for their children to do well academically in English, through maintenance of first language and cultural heritage at home (Caplan, Choy, & Whitmore, 1992).

Other creative solutions to support systems for refugees from war have developed in diverse school settings. Hmong families originally from Southeast Asia who have emigrated to Fresno, California, and Minneapolis-St. Paul, Minnesota, have come to value schooling in Hmong and English as an important means for their children to succeed in school. Their home language was not formerly a written language, but bilingual teachers in these school districts have created biliteracy materials for the early grades in Hmong by developing authentic literature from family stories. These support systems have enhanced the Hmong students' confidence and success in U.S. schools (López, 2000).

Another trend of recent decades is that second-generation Vietnamese families on the west coast of the U.S. who were starting to lose their heritage language are requesting Vietnamese-English dual language programs for their children. With the passage of time, the emotional trauma of the past is being healed as these families see the benefits for their children in becoming bilingual adults, reconnecting to their heritage while preparing for the global workplace of the 21st century.

Emigration from an economically depressed region. For the last several decades, unprecedented numbers of adults and young people have been arriving in the U.S. from Central America and Mexico. Their story is told in documentaries such as *Harvest of Empire: The Untold Story of Latinos in America* (Getzels, López, &

González, 2012) and in the book *Enrique's Journey* (Nazario, 2014). Climate change is bringing more extremes in weather and natural disasters in Central America, causing crops to fail and the infrastructure for transportation, health, and other basic services to be disrupted. In addition, economic conditions, drug trade, and violence have led to extremely difficult living conditions, and many families go north seeking safety and work. Among this group are unaccompanied Central American children and youth (estimated at more than 100,000 arrivals in the U.S. each year)—often searching for their parents or other family members who emigrated earlier.

Those who successfully connect with family members in the U.S. are able to start a new life, and first- and second-generation immigrants have contributed greatly to their communities and their new country. Dual language classes can provide the school context for these students to succeed by making up for lost school time through their native language while also acquiring English through the school curriculum. With time, they can reach grade-level achievement and full English proficiency when the dual language program is continued throughout middle and high school, Grades K–12. Newcomers (new immigrants) belong in the dual language program, whatever their age.

Socioeconomic status. Another social factor is the influence of poverty on school achievement. In education research of the 1960s and 1970s, socioeconomic status was identified as one of the most powerful variables influencing students' achievement in schools. For many decades, Title I federal funds have provided for individualized instruction in language arts and mathematics for students of low-income background who are not doing well in school. A common approach to teaching these students has been to assume that they are best taught through a carefully structured, sequenced, basic skills approach. After three decades of research on this type of schooling, education researchers have concluded that simplified texts and discrete-skills teaching isolated from meaningful contexts actually widens the gap in achievement between middle-class and low-income students as they move into cognitively and academically more complex material with each succeeding grade level (Cloud, Genesee, & Hamayan, 2000; Collier, 1992; Cummins, 1996; Valdés, Menken, & Castro, 2015).

In contrast, when students experience natural language development, exploring authentic literature and cognitively complex curricular activities through balanced literacy approaches, they are able to achieve on or above grade level. These instructional approaches—along with instructional strategies that intentionally and explicitly address language and culture—are the standard for dual language teaching (Beeman & Urow, 2013). We have found in many of our studies comparing students of low socioeconomic status in dual language to those not in dual language that the dual language teaching practices significantly improve student success. When in a well-implemented program for many years, dual language students from poverty consistently outscore their peers not attending dual language classes and completely close the gap, reaching grade-level achievement.

Language minority students show great variety in their cultural, linguistic, and socioeconomic backgrounds and in their current circumstances. Included in this group are recent immigrants who are well-educated middle-or upper-class members who must now reestablish themselves professionally and who seek educational and economic means of restoring their former income levels as quickly as possible. Others who are not as well educated seek to enhance their education in their host country as a means of faster upward mobility. Still others may find themselves unable to do this because of life circumstances and continue in a lower socioeconomic status. Because of these variations in experience, socioeconomic status may not affect language minorities' academic achievement in the same ways as for native English speakers. Among many language minorities, the desire for education as one key to upward mobility has provided the fuel to overcome poverty.

We see this pattern in our longitudinal studies examining both English learners and native English speakers, comparing groups of students in dual language classes to comparable groups not in dual language. From our studies conducted over 30 years in many school districts of all regions of the U.S., we found that dual language classes reduced the negative influence of poverty on student achievement, from 18% to less than 5%. Poverty is still a powerful variable overall, but dual language classes can largely overcome the power of this social influence. Schools that provide a strong bilingual/bicultural, academically rich context for instruction can succeed in helping all students achieve at high levels, regardless of their socioeconomic background (Collier & Thomas, 2009, pp. 82-83; Thomas & Collier, 2002).

> **Figure 5.2**
>
> **Dual Language Programs and African American Students from Thomas and Collier Research in North Carolina (statewide, 2009-2014) and in Houston, TX (districtwide, 1995-2002)**
>
> - They receive an enriched (gifted) education rather than a remedial education.
> - They become trilingual—community dialect, standard English, and partner language.
> - Their school attendance improves.
> - Their engagement with schooling increases.
> - Their achievement (as tested in both English and the partner language) greatly improves.
> - Their levels of cognitive development increase.
> - Their rate of cognitive development accelerates.
> - Their achievement gap with other groups is greatly reduced.
> - Any negative impact of low-income family background on test scores is greatly reduced.
> - English learners and native English speakers derive more meaning from lessons taught through second-language strategies.
>
> Copyright © 2010-2017, W.P. Thomas and V.P. Collier. All rights reserved.

African American students. In Chapter 2, we introduced the intriguing results of our findings in Houston, Texas, and the state of North Carolina regarding the advantages that dual language classes provide for all native English speakers—but especially for African American students of low-income background. Analyzing all North Carolina state test scores over a 3-year period, we found that African American students attending dual language classes strongly outperformed their peers not in dual language, making just as much dramatic progress in closing the achievement gap as English learners were making. By the middle school years, the African American students of low-income background in dual language from kindergarten on were two grades ahead of those not in dual language, a phenomenal achievement. From interviews with students and staff, we can see that some of the impact of the dual language program is due to the improved social, emotional, and cultural context for learning.

African American students attending dual language classes perceive the program as a gifted curriculum—they feel privileged, respected, and valued. These students develop high self-esteem as they master expansion of their second language for each grade level, plus the acquisition of standard English, while becoming more perceptive of the relationships between the dialectal variations that they experience in their community and at school. They come to value and celebrate the many variations of language use as they see that there are regional varieties of the partner language and English. Their high self-esteem also develops through the cross-cultural perspectives that the students acquire as they affirm and celebrate the multiple ethnicities of those who speak, read, and write both the partner language and English. They see their world from a more global perspective, including the opportunities that await them as they mature into young adults (Thomas & Collier, 2014).

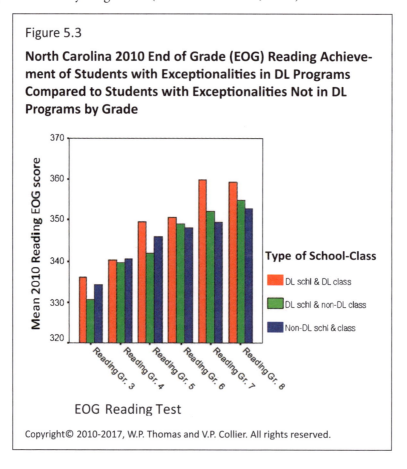

Figure 5.3

North Carolina 2010 End of Grade (EOG) Reading Achievement of Students with Exceptionalities in DL Programs Compared to Students with Exceptionalities Not in DL Programs by Grade

Copyright© 2010-2017, W.P. Thomas and V.P. Collier. All rights reserved.

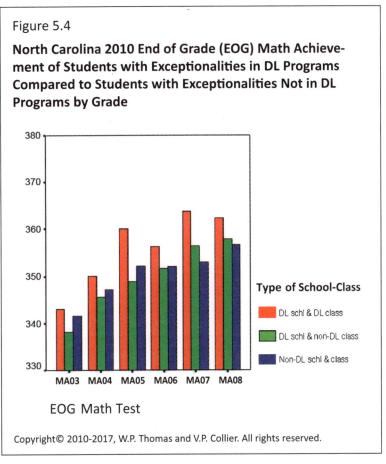

Figure 5.4

North Carolina 2010 End of Grade (EOG) Math Achievement of Students with Exceptionalities in DL Programs Compared to Students with Exceptionalities Not in DL Programs by Grade

Copyright© 2010-2017, W.P. Thomas and V.P. Collier. All rights reserved.

Students with special needs. School populations also include students who are assessed as needing extra support because of physical challenges, learning disabilities, autism, and other categories of exceptionality. In the analyses that we conducted for the state of North Carolina, we found that the dual language programs throughout the state include some students with special needs. We were able to confirm the research findings already established in Canada that students with special needs can thrive in dual language classes (Bruck, 1982; Genesee, 1987; Genesee, Paradis, & Crago, 2004; Lindholm-Leary & Genesee, 2010). In fact, we found the special needs dual language students doing better than their peers not in dual language (Thomas & Collier, 2014). Clearly it does not harm these students to study through two languages; instead, it enhances their success in school when parents choose to place their children in the dual language program.

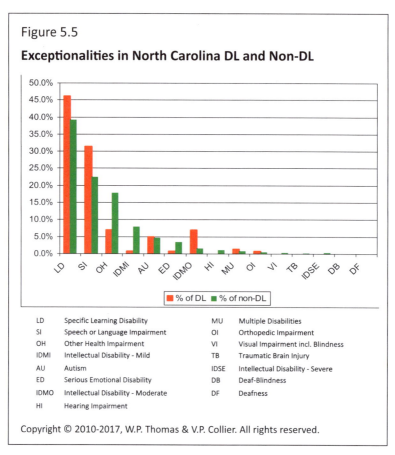

Figure 5.5

Exceptionalities in North Carolina DL and Non-DL

LD	Specific Learning Disability
SI	Speech or Language Impairment
OH	Other Health Impairment
IDMI	Intellectual Disability - Mild
AU	Autism
ED	Serious Emotional Disability
IDMO	Intellectual Disability - Moderate
HI	Hearing Impairment
MU	Multiple Disabilities
OI	Orthopedic Impairment
VI	Visual Impairment incl. Blindness
TB	Traumatic Brain Injury
IDSE	Intellectual Disability - Severe
DB	Deaf-Blindness
DF	Deafness

Copyright © 2010-2017, W.P. Thomas & V.P. Collier. All rights reserved.

Addressing the needs of all students. Because dual language teachers have often experienced multiple social and cultural contexts in their own lifetimes, they tend to be more sensitive to those students who need extra emotional support in the initial years of schooling. Additionally, with their ESL and bilingual endorsements, these teachers often bring more varied instructional strategies to the classroom that address the sociocultural aspects of learning. The social and emotional support that students receive in a dual language classroom is powerful, as is the ongoing cognitive stimulation and development. Whatever the students' circumstances, they feel empowered when they join their peers studying the curriculum through two languages.

Conclusion

Social relationships between groups or individual students can sometimes have strong, powerful influences within the school. Majority-minority relations and social class differences mirror societal patterns of discrimination and prejudice. Humans tend to create social hierarchies based on perceptions (or misperceptions) of groups or individuals (McKay & Wong, 2000). By creating a school culture different from the society surrounding the school, staff and students can shape a new sociocultural context within the school, and that is precisely what dual language classes are designed to do.

Two-way dual language classes bring together English speakers and English learners, students from poverty and from the middle class, and students of varying ethnic backgrounds and cultures. Within this mix, roles are equalized. The classroom tasks require cooperation to accomplish the assignments. No longer are the native English speakers experiencing advantages because they speak the only language of the curriculum. Instead, both groups are "experts." Each group shares the role of leadership when the instructional work is done in their native language. They each help facilitate their peers' second language acquisition and access to the curriculum. They teach each other. In fact, this is a distinguishing characteristic of two-way dual language education.

Many sociological studies in education of the past several decades found patterns of differential treatment for minority groups in U.S. schools that led to denial of access to education services provided for the majority. These types of studies identified practices such as counseling minorities into non-academic tracks, ability grouping, and providing pullout services that segregate students from the mainstream (Valdés, 2001; Valenzuela, 1999). Dual language schooling works to resolve these issues, encouraging inclusion and integration of students. Transitional bilingual education resulted in segregated classes provided only for English learners, which led to social isolation of these students. The shift from transitional bilingual classes towards dual language schooling for all has resulted in dual language becoming an integral part of the curricular mainstream in many schools and districts.

Heterogeneous school populations are common these days in U.S. schools. Cummins and other authors have used the term "empowerment" to symbolize the struggles embodied in each group's access to education and overall success in life (Cummins, 2000). Empowerment includes shared decision making among parents, teachers, students, and administrators. Empowerment in heterogeneous contexts also implies developing curricula, instructional methods, assessment practices, and administrative structures that serve all student groups equally effectively. This means providing meaningful, high-quality, interdisciplinary, academic problem solving from a multicultural, global perspective. That is what dual language schools do very well. Schools do not have to be limited by existing societal patterns. Dual language curricula help students to understand sociocultural differences between groups and individuals so that students come to value and respect each other. As young adults, dual language students are better prepared for the very diverse workplace of the 21st century.

Chapter Six
Dual Language Programs as a Vehicle for School System Reform

School leaders are eager to discover educational programs that are truly effective for diverse populations, while saving escalating costs. In the past, our biggest concern in U.S. schools was the continuing isolation from the educational mainstream of minorities, low-income groups, English learners, and students with special needs. U.S. educators created special programs intended to serve these students more effectively with specialized teachers and small class sizes, but many of these students continued to be low-achieving and segregated for significant periods of time from students in the "standard curriculum." It is time for a dramatic change!

As we stated in the beginning of Chapter 1, dual language education is the standard curriculum taught through two languages. It is not a separate, segregated program—dual language is the mainstream. Dual language classes are designed for all students, and dual language teachers are trained to work with very heterogeneous groups of students. No longer is it necessary to send individual students out for specialized pullout services. Students of many different backgrounds thrive in dual language classes. And, surprisingly, when dual language programs are carefully planned, they can be very cost-effective in comparison to pullout services. Let's examine some of the features of this innovative school program that bring major changes to the ways that educators approach schooling.

Envisioning Central Administration Coordination in Your School District

In states with no statewide initiatives to encourage the implementation of dual language programs, school districts often hear about dual language through contact with neighboring school districts. At the central administrative level, those initiating the discussion frequently include the department heads for English learner services and world languages. In the past, it was unusual for these two offices to work together since they perceived their mission as independent from each other because they served different students. Those organizing foreign language classes (now called world languages) prepared for native-English-speaking students who were starting study of another language at secondary level, while the school leaders in charge of bilingual/ESOL services viewed their role as serving only English learners.

Nowadays dual language programs unite these two divisions and bring these school leaders into the kind of dialogues that occur among all curricular supervisors—for example, language arts and literacy, mathematics, social studies, science, special education—for all grade levels PK–12. This changes the way everything is done at the central administrative level, potentially leading to systemic reform. This coordination can occur only when the superintendent, chief academic officer, and all other upper administrative leadership, as well as all school board members, understand and fully support the dual language program.

Figure 6.1

What Does "Well-implemented Dual Language" Mean?

Dual language programs have the greatest educational potential of all the program alternatives, and thus, they are most affected by how well the program is actually carried out. Poor or incomplete implementation leads to lower achievement, while well-implemented DL shows very large educational effects for all participating groups. So, the degree and quality of DL implementation really does matter!

These are characteristics observed in well-implemented dual language programs:

- **Administrators at both school and district levels** (superintendent, school board, central office staff, and principals) **fully support the DL program** by providing the financial and administrative resources to hire qualified teachers who are academically proficient in the languages of instruction and to choose high-quality classroom materials and equipment.
- **The DL principal must fully understand and support every aspect of the DL program, as the program's greatest advocate.**
- **The program's characteristics closely follow the specifications of the DL model chosen.** All staff fully understand the research-based rationale for key program features, the non-negotiable components of the model, and why these are important to program success. Administrators make sure that these are actually carried out in DL classrooms.
- **Careful attention is given to instructional time in EACH of the two languages,** with deep proficiency development of BOTH languages throughout the academic curriculum.
- **Regular DL program planning meetings are scheduled** at which staff can discuss what is working well and what might need to be changed through collaborative decision making.
- **All bilingual and English-speaking teachers work closely together, both creatively and collaboratively.** Teachers who are assigned as team-teaching partners appreciate and value each other, and together, they plan the strategies that will lead to the desired instructional outcomes.
- **Educators make thoughtful choices of valid and reliable assessment instruments** for BOTH languages across the curriculum for continuous program evaluation of important program outcomes.
- **The school district provides high-quality and ongoing staff development** in research-based, effective practices for DL teachers and administrators.

Copyright © 2013-2017, W.P. Thomas and V.P. Collier. All rights reserved.

Through this coordinated effort, financial and logistical support is provided by all departments for hiring bilingual staff, acquiring high-quality curricular and library resources in the two languages of the program, and providing dual language professional development for all staff. For example, when new textbook adoption occurs, the decision is made jointly by all, making sure that similar or parallel materials are available in the non-English language for the dual language classes. In addition, support is required from the research and evaluation office regarding thoughtful choices in valid assessment instruments in both languages and ongoing longitudinal evaluation of the program. In the long term, the elementary school dual language program is best evaluated by middle school outcomes at the end of sixth and eighth grades, when the assessment instruments measure higher cognitive attainment across the curriculum for Grades PK–8. This allows for the development of well-founded conclusions about how well the elementary schools prepared their students for the more academically rigorous middle school years, using more difficult tests than in elementary school.

In geographical regions that have had no previous experience with dual language or transitional bilingual schooling, the program sometimes starts with one visionary principal in one school leading the way. But even in these school districts, central office coordination is required because once the other principals and parents see how successful the program is, dual language services tend to expand to other schools in the district because parents demand it.

In states with bilingual legislative mandates for schooling English learners and in large urban school districts, dual language programs are sometimes implemented and expanded at an astounding pace across many schools. The general pattern for opening dual language classes is to start with the early grades (PK–K or K–1 or just one of these grade levels) and then add one grade level each year to the program. The non-English language chosen is the language represented by the largest group of English learners enrolled in the school district. In the U.S., that is almost always Spanish. Spanish-English programs are very popular with English-speaking parents, so it is usually not difficult to fill the English-speaking portion of class enrollment, leading to the need to continue expanding the program to more classes and more schools.

Large urban school districts must also plan and hire the bilingual staff to serve their other large language groups as soon as they can provide the resources, resulting in searches for high quality curricular materials in the less commonly taught languages in the U.S. The challenges increase with each grade level, as staff work to find curricular materials in the non-English languages that are academically equivalent to the English curriculum. Implementing the program one grade per year buys some time to find qualified bilingual staff and search for high-quality curricular materials. All of these program implementation decisions need to be made jointly by all curricular leaders, with the experienced dual language coordinators leading the way.

Once central administrative staff understand and value this mainstream program taught through two languages, they become supportive participants in the decision making. Central administrators will then begin to experience the dramatic improvement in their school district's student achievement patterns, especially for groups served less well in the past. The coordination required across subjects and grade levels becomes creative, sustained, efficient, and productive. The initial challenges turn into solutions that resolve issues for diverse staff and students (Collier & Thomas, 2014).

Principals as Dual Language Leaders

The principal of a dual language school is the key to the success of the program. This instructional leader needs to be extremely knowledgeable about how well-implemented dual language education works. Without the principal's full support for high-quality and consistent implementation, the program may not flourish and those high scores on the tests desired by the whole school community will not be realized. Working in close coordination with the district's director of dual language, the principal is responsible for hiring highly qualified and academically proficient bilingual teachers and school staff and making curricular and assessment decisions. Once the dual language model is chosen, the instructional team then plans the campus schedule that best follows the guidelines for the model and allows staff ample planning time for the necessary collaboration that occurs in dual language classes. Critical principal tasks include providing appropriate professional development opportunities, monitoring instruction for appropriate bilingual teacher evaluation, and developing a means of ensuring that all components of the dual language program are working well. In order for the dual language program to thrive and grow, it is also necessary to organize parent meetings to explain the dual language program to new parents, to answer parent questions that arise as the school year progresses, and to enlist parent support in attracting other families who may be searching for a uniquely enriched instructional program for their children. The school principal oversees everything that goes on within the school. These additional responsibilities ensure the success of the dual language program.

> **Figure 6.2**
>
> **Planning Considerations for Dual Language Principals**
>
> - Address all decisions for English learners as a whole school staff from an enrichment perspective, rather than as a separately staffed, remedial program within your school.
> - Hire bilingual/ESL staff who are dual certified with every hiring opportunity created through retirements, transfers, or new teaching allocations.
> - Include planning time for teaching teams in the master schedule.
> - Make sure that regular faculty meetings include ongoing planning for the services provided to English learners.
> - Provide ongoing professional development for all staff that supports their understanding of second language acquisition, cross-cultural awareness, and instructional strategies that enhance English learners' access to the academic curriculum.
> - Provide staff planning time and funding for acquiring curricular materials and developing a wide variety of hands-on, discovery-learning materials.
> - Conduct effective monitoring of instruction for appropriate bilingual teacher evaluation.
> - Be prepared to respond to parents' questions and concerns by becoming knowledgeable about key points regarding the second language acquisition process and the importance of continuing first language development.
> - Let your decisions reflect the high value placed on bilingualism and intercultural knowledge building by all students and staff at your school.
>
> Copyright © 2011-2017, W.P. Thomas and V.P. Collier. All rights reserved.

This may at first seem overwhelming to a new dual language principal, but the experienced principals who have served in this role say that it is exhilarating and extremely rewarding. (We encourage you to read our book on dual language administration, written by 26 authors, most of whom have served as principals of dual language schools—Collier & Thomas, 2014.) From the perspective of systemic reform, traditional leadership roles are transformed in several major ways for the principal of a dual language school, solving problems that have overwhelmed more traditional schools.

Perhaps the most dramatic and visible change is the way students behave in the school. The dual language program actually lessens the load that principals typically experience, since behavior management can often be an overwhelming chore in very diverse schools. The cross-cultural mix in the teaching staff and their multilingual communication with the students bring a more peaceful clarity and resolution to interactions among faculty and students. For example, when analyzing data from the entire state of North Carolina, in comparison to students not in dual language, we found that behavioral referrals were greatly reduced among students attending dual language classes (Thomas & Collier, 2014). From all research findings on dual language, we find that the two most dramatic outcomes are increased student engagement with learning (resulting in less misbehavior) and higher levels of cognitive/academic development for all student groups. This program dramatically increases student achievement, with the greatest gains among students of low-income background and English learners. The dual language program raises the school's achievement scores, lessening the principal's anxiety about low performance and failing to meet the state's criteria for school success. Accountability has been a huge issue of the past couple of decades in U.S. schools. Dual language schooling can be a very important remedy and, in the long term, solves many of the problems that currently perplex school district administrators.

Dual language programs require fundamental changes in the English-only learning environments of U.S. schools of the past. The new vision is to graduate students who are bilingual and biliterate, able to navigate the multicultural adult world of the 21st century. This means changes in teaching practices, curricular materials, accountability, and assessments—leading to systemic reform in each individual school and throughout the school district. To successfully negotiate these shifts, instructional leaders need to reach out to and visit other schools and school districts implementing dual language classes, to attend professional conferences and regional professional development sessions focused on dual language, and to identify support organizations within the community and beyond, including resources from other countries where the non-English language is spoken. Most important is for the principal to help develop local parent support as the program matures. This support can include advocacy for the program, with parent leadership taking responsibility for helping to meet the needs of different parent groups in the school and providing input for the ongoing refinement of the dual language program.

Changes in Teaching Practices

Team teaching. Another major systemic change that dual language classes bring to a school is the concept of team teaching. In regions where many teacher applicants are academically proficient in the two languages of the dual language program, each class may be self-contained with one teacher providing the instruction through both languages. But this is rare. More often, administrators spend a lot of time searching for qualified, licensed bilingual teachers. Given the current shortage of bilingual teachers, team teaching is a dynamic solution until a future time when U.S. schools have graduated enough dual language students who come back to be teachers. To be cost-effective, the two teachers are assigned two classes, thus maintaining the school's student-teacher ratio. The two partner teachers trade their two classes back and forth, following a well-designed curricular plan, so that all students have an equal number of curricular experiences in both languages and all grade-level subjects are covered. English-speaking teachers are an important component of the program; thus, they should be reassured that they will not lose their jobs! Only half of the teaching staff needs to be proficiently bilingual, and since the program is grown grade by grade in successive years, principals may hire a few additional bilingual staff each year by filling positions that are available through retirements and reassignments.

Team teaching makes more efficient and productive use of the teaching staff in each building. At the same time, teachers need more staff development support and planning time to make team teaching in dual language programs work. First, the teachers who are partnered must get along together. Both the bilingual teachers and the monolingual English teachers must be well trained in second language techniques for making meaning and developing language in all subjects of the curriculum, since both teachers in the partnership will have students who are second language learners. If existing ESL staff are used for the English positions, the ESL staff must be academically proficient in English and double-licensed to teach both ESL and the curricular subjects being taught in English. Likewise, the bilingual teachers must be academically proficient in the non-English language, schooled in second language techniques, and licensed to teach the curricular subjects being taught in that partner language.

When team teaching is flowing smoothly, each teacher adds to the cognitive level of instruction by teaching in his/her most developed and cognitively mature language. This becomes increasingly important in the upper grades as the cognitive level of instruction increases. Students respond by becoming more engaged with learning because they are stimulated by the different multicultural perspectives of the two teachers. To keep up with their lessons the students need to pay very close attention, especially when the instruction is in a language that they know less well. The authenticity of the lessons is reinforced by each teacher's knowledge and perspectives from other linguistic and cultural life experiences that the teachers share with their students. The bicultural curriculum takes on new meaning, expanding students' awareness and preparing them for adult life in multicultural contexts.

Figure 6.3
What Does Well-implemented and Effective DL Instruction Look Like?

- DL teachers know that they always have second language learners among their students, so they use many scaffolding strategies:
  - mime and nonverbal gestures;
  - pictures, drawings, and graphic organizers;
  - songs and chanting;
  - anchor charts;
  - puppets, acting, and movement;
  - Smart Boards, video, interactive programs; and
  - whatever it takes to get across the "what, how, and why" of lessons for heterogeneous classes.
- Teachers powerfully plan and utilize cooperative learning strategies:
  - Small groups allow for more focused time with individual students for differentiated instruction.
  - Cognitive and academic outcomes are stimulated by small group work.
  - Teachers encourage much more student-to-student interaction and less teacher-to-student interaction—students learn language by using it!
- Teachers plan instructional activities across all levels of Bloom's Taxonomy, rather than emphasizing low-level skills and short-term instructional outcomes.
- Teachers utilize meaningful, real-world problem solving; creative projects; varied activities; authentic literature; cognitively challenging tasks; and stimulating learning experiences—and they do so across the curriculum.
- Teachers use varied work groupings, such as pairs, groups of four, learning centers, and whole-class instruction.
- Teachers de-emphasize lecturing. When used, direct instruction is intentional and of short duration. Routines and procedures are modeled and consistent.
- Teachers show sensitivity to cross-cultural issues and provide emotional support for all.
- Teachers encourage students to actively participate as they are able, regardless of the language of instruction (student's first or second language).
- Teachers and fellow students provide intentional and explicit non-verbal and verbal clues to meaning for both content and language.

Copyright © 2017, W.P. Thomas and V.P. Collier. All rights reserved.

Innovative teaching. Another systemic change that dual language programs bring to school systems is the development of bold, new strategies for teaching. Dual language teachers have to be extremely creative, skilled, and knowledgeable to effectively teach the curricular material to the students who are not yet proficient in the language of instruction. Several things happen. All kinds of extra clues to meaning are developed by both the teacher and students as they explore curricular content.

These can include pantomime, artistry, gestures and other nonverbal cues; songs, including rap and many other musical expressions; real-life materials; technologies such as Smart boards, video, interactive programs; puppets, dance and movement; chants and jingles; visuals and graphic organizers ... the possibilities are endless. Our research is finding that these second-language teaching strategies help all students better understand the meaning of the lessons, so that students who struggled in the past are thriving in dual language classes. Students who used to be pulled out for individual or small-group help are doing better without pullout services. This is another way that dual language programs are more cost-effective.

Furthermore, cooperative learning, which is a mainstay of all good teaching, is an essential and required element of dual language classes. Since language is best acquired from peers of the same age, dual language classes include lots of peer work in bilingual pairs and small groups that mix students by language background and ability. During lessons in the partner language, the students who are native speakers of that language are the peer experts, helping to mentor their peers in the group projects conducted in class. The same process occurs during English time, with native-English-speaking students serving as peer experts. As both language groups grow in proficiency, they continue to teach each other, expanding their academic vocabulary and knowledge, grade by grade.

As you visit dual language classes, you should see much more than an emphasis on low-level skills and short-term objectives. In fact, you should see evidence of problem solving, creative projects, greatly varied activities, high-level thinking, and stimulating learning taking place, all experienced through both languages and within a multicultural perspective. Dual language classes are not silent. They are busy, interactive, thoughtful learning contexts where students are so engaged with their work that they don't even notice the visitors in their room.

Conclusion

In this book, we have considered many reasons to implement dual language schooling and to carry it off well. The United States is ready for this big change. U.S. schools continue to serve very diverse student populations. The world is changing and global interconnections surround us in all fields of endeavor. When our schools prepare our students for a highly charged, fast-paced, 21st century environment that will continue to change and even redefine itself rapidly, we will be serving our students and communities well. We have the tools, the resources, and the experience needed now to transform our school systems into thoughtfully designed, more efficient, more productive educational experiences taught through two languages. Dual language schooling is for everyone. We are inspired educational leaders with visions for the future—let's make this happen!

Resources

After reading *Why Dual Language Schooling,* a school community may be inspired to take the next steps in planning or strengthening their dual language program implementation.

School communities committed to successfully implementing and sustaining a dual language education program often need assistance with that implementation. Fortunately, there are a number of established service providers who are ready to partner with your school community by providing program and professional development services. Some partners are able to provide program planning retreats, others can train and support dual language teachers, and still others may have resources to share in research, community engagement, and advocacy. Here is a list of some of the most effective dual language school community partners in the country.

1. Association for Two-Way Dual Language Education: *www.atdle.org*
2. BUENO Multicultural Education Center: *www.buenocenter.org*
3. California Association for Bilingual Education: *www.gocabe.org*
4. Center for Applied Linguistics: *www.cal.org*
5. Center for Teaching for Biliteracy: *www.teachingforbiliteracy.com*
6. Dual Language Education of New Mexico: *www.dlenm.org*
7. Massachusetts Association for Bilingual Education: *www.massmabe.org*
8. Paridad Education Consulting: *www.paridad.us*

Figures

Figure 1.1: The Most Important Research Findings About Dual Language Education..... 2

Figure 1.2: Longitudinal Gap Closure for Grade 3-7 Cohort................................... 3

Figure 1.3: The Cognitive Advantages of Being Bilingual 5

Figure 1.4: Why Dual Language? The Research Rationale................................... 13

Figure 1.5: Important World Languages 15

Figure 2.1: Reasons to Enroll in Dual Language Classes 18

Figure 2.2: States Offering Biliteracy Seals at High School Graduation 20

Figure 2.3: Advantages of Dual Language Inclusion... 24

Figure 3.1: First Language Acquisition and Cognitive Development are Closely Related... 34

Figure 3.2: Dual Language Students 37

Figure 4.1: Stephen Krashen's Natural Order of ESL Morpheme Acquisition (Krashen, 1981).. 41

Figure 4.2: Pattern of Acquisition of Grammar Structures in Second Language 43

Figure 5.1: Examples of Social and Cultural Processes in Second Language Acquisition 56

Figure 5.2: Dual Language Programs and African American Students from Thomas and Collier Research in North Carolina (statewide, 2009-2014) and in Houston, TX (districtwide, 1995-2002).. 61

Figure 5.3: North Carolina 2010 End of Grade (EOG) Reading Achievement of Students with Exceptionalities in DL Programs Compared to Students with Exceptionalities Not in DL Programs by Grade 62

Figure 5.4: North Carolina 2010 End of Grade (EOG) Math Achievement of Students with Exceptionalities in DL Programs Compared to Students with Exceptionalities Not in DL Programs by Grade 63

Figure 5.5: Exceptionalities in North Carolina DL and Non-DL............................. 64

Figure 6.1: What Does "Well-implemented Dual Language" Mean? 68

Figure 6.2: Planning Considerations for Dual Language Principals...................... 71

Figure 6.3: What Does Well-implemented and Effective DL Instruction Look Like? 74

For access to the figures in this book, please contact DLeNM/Fuente Press at *publications@dlenm.org*.

References

Aikio-Puoskari, U. (2009). The ethnic revival, language and education of the Sámi, an Indigenous people, in three Nordic countries (Finland, Norway and Sweden). In T. Skutnabb-Kangas, R. Phillipson, A.K. Hohanty, & M. Panda (Eds.), *Social justice through multilingual education* (pp. 238-262). Bristol, UK: Multilingual Matters.

Baker, C. (2011). *Foundations of bilingual education and bilingualism* (5th ed.). Bristol, UK: Multilingual Matters.

Beeman, K., & Urow, C. (2013). *Teaching for biliteracy: Strengthening bridges between languages.* Philadelphia: Caslon.

Bialystok, E. (2011). Reshaping the mind: The benefits of bilingualism. *Canadian Journal of Experimental Psychology, 65*(4), 229-235.

Bruck, M. (1982). Language disabled children: Performance in an additive bilingual education program. *Applied Psycholinguistics, 3,* 45-60.

California Department of Education. (1986). *Beyond language: Social and cultural factors in schooling language minority students.* Sacramento, CA: California Department of Education.

Caplan, N., Choy, M.H., & Whitmore, J.K. (1992). Indochinese refugee families and academic achievement. *Scientific American, 266*(2), 36-42.

Castañeda v. Pickard, 648 F.2d 989 5th Cir. (1981).

Center for Applied Linguistics. (2017). *Two-way immersion directory.* Washington, DC: Center for Applied Linguistics. http://www.cal.org/twi/directory

Cloud, N., Genesee, F., & Hamayan, E. (2000). *Dual language instruction: A handbook for enriched education.* Boston: Thomson-Heinle.

Coelho, E. (1994). Social integration of immigrant and refugee children. In F. Genesee (Ed.), *Educating second language children* (pp. 301-327). Cambridge: Cambridge University Press.

Collier, V.P. (1987). Age and rate of acquisition of second language for academic purposes. *TESOL Quarterly, 21,* 617-641.

Collier, V.P. (1988). *The effect of age on acquisition of a second language for school.* Washington, DC: National Clearinghouse for English Language Acquisition.

Collier, V.P. (1992). The Canadian bilingual immersion debate: A synthesis of research findings. *Studies in Second Language Acquisition, 14,* 87-97.

Collier, V.P. (1995). *Promoting academic success for ESL students: Understanding second language acquisition for school.* Elizabeth, NJ: New Jersey Teachers of English to Speakers of Other Languages-Bilingual Educators.

Collier, V.P., & Thomas, W.P. (1989). How quickly can immigrants become proficient in school English? *Journal of Educational Issues of Language Minority Students, 5,* 26-38.

Collier, V.P., & Thomas, W.P. (2009). *Educating English learners for a transformed world.* Albuquerque, NM: Dual Language Education of New Mexico-Fuente Press. Print and electronic editions.

Collier, V.P., & Thomas, W.P. (2013). *La educación de los estudiantes de inglés para un mundo en constante transformación.* Albuquerque, NM: Dual Language Education of New Mexico-Fuente Press. Electronic edition.

Collier, V.P., & Thomas, W.P. (2014). *Creating dual language schools for a transformed world: Administrators speak.* Albuquerque, NM: Dual Language Education of New Mexico-Fuente Press. Print and electronic editions.

Collier, V.P., & Thomas, W.P. (2017). Validating the power of bilingual schooling: Thirty-two years of large-scale, longitudinal research. *Annual Review of Applied Linguistics.* Cambridge: Cambridge University Press.

Cummins, J. (1979). Cognitive/academic language proficiency, linguistic interdependence, the optimal age question, and some other matters. *Working Papers on Bilingualism,* No. 19 (pp. 197-205). Toronto: Ontario Institute for Studies in Education.

Cummins, J. (1981). The role of primary language development in promoting educational success for language minority students. In California State Department of Education (Ed.), *Schooling and language minority students: A theoretical framework.* Los Angeles: California State University, Evaluation, Dissemination, and Assessment Center.

Cummins, J. (1991). Interdependence of first- and second-language proficiency in bilingual children. In E. Bialystok (Ed.), *Language processing in bilingual children* (pp. 70-89). Cambridge: Cambridge University Press.

Cummins, J. (2000). *Language, power and pedagogy: Bilingual children in the crossfire.* Bristol, UK: Multilingual Matters.

Cummins, J. (2001). *Negotiating identities: Education for empowerment in a diverse society* (2nd ed.). Los Angeles: California Association for Bilingual Education.

Ellis, R. (1985). *Understanding second language acquisition.* Oxford: Oxford University Press.

Ellis, R. (1994). *The study of second language acquisition.* Oxford: Oxford University Press.

Escamilla, K., Hopewell, S., Butvilofsky, S., Sparrow, W., Soltero-González, L., Ruiz-Figueroa, O., & Escamilla, M. (2014). *Biliteracy from the start: Literacy squared in action.* Philadelphia: Caslon.

Francis, N., & Reyhner, J. (2002). *Language and literacy teaching for Indigenous education: A bilingual approach.* Bristol, UK: Multilingual Matters.

Freeman, R. (2004). *Building on community bilingualism.* Philadelphia: Caslon.

Freeman, Y.S., Freeman, D.E., & Mercuri, S.P. (2005). *Dual language essentials for teachers and administrators.* Portsmouth, NH: Heinemann.

García, O., Skutnabb-Kangas, T., & Torres-Guzmán, M.E. (Eds.). (2006). *Imagining multilingual schools: Languages in education and glocalization.* Bristol, UK: Multilingual Matters.

Genesee, F. (1987). *Learning through two languages: Studies of immersion and bilingual education.* New York: Newbury House.

Genesee, F., Paradis, J., & Crago, M.B. (2004). *Dual language development and disorders: A handbook on bilingualism and second language learning.* Baltimore: Paul H. Brookes Publishing.

Getzels, P., López, E. (Directors), & González, J. (Author). (2012). *Harvest of empire: The untold story of Latinos in America* [Documentary]. United States: Onyx Films.

Grosjean, F. (2010). *Bilingual: Life and reality.* Cambridge, MA: Harvard University Press.

Hakuta, K. (1986). *Mirror of language: The debate on bilingualism.* New York: Basic Books.

Hamayan, E., Genesee, F., & Cloud, N. (2013). *Dual language instruction from A to Z: Practical guidance for teachers and administrators.* Portsmouth, NH: Heinemann.

Hudelson, S. (1994). Literacy development of second language children. In F. Genesee (Ed.), *Educating second language children* (pp. 129-158). Cambridge: Cambridge University Press.

Kagan, S. (2013). *Cooperative learning.* San Clemente, CA: Kagan Cooperative Learning.

Krashen, S.D. (1981). *Second language acquisition and second language learning.* Oxford: Pergamon.

Lau v. Nichols, 414 U.S. 563 (1974).

Lindholm-Leary, K. (2001). *Dual language education.* Bristol, UK: Multilingual Matters.

Lindholm-Leary, K., & Genesee, F. (2010). Alternative educational programs for English learners. In *Improving Education for English Learners: Research-based approaches* (pp. 323-382). Sacramento, CA: California Department of Education.

Long, M. (1988). Maturational constraints on language development. *Studies in Second Language Acquisition, 12,* 251-285.

López, M.G. (2000). The language situation of the Hmong, Khmer, and Laotian communities in the United States. In S.L. McKay & S.C. Wong (Eds.), *New immigrants in the United States* (pp. 232-262). Cambridge: Cambridge University Press.

Lyons, J. (Curator). (2014). *Scoop It! Benefits of bilingualism.* Albuquerque, NM: Dual Language Education of New Mexico. Retrieved from http://www.scoop.it/t/benefits-of-bilingualism

McCarty, T.L. (2009). Empowering Indigenous languages – What can be learned from Native American experiences? In T. Skutnabb-Kangas, R. Phillipson, A.K. Mohanty, & M. Panda (Eds.), *Social justice through multilingual educa-*

tion (pp. 125-139). Bristol, UK: Multilingual Matters.

McCarty, T.L., Romero, M.E., & Zepeda, O. (2006). Reimagining multilingual America: Lessons from Native American youth. In O. García, T. Skutnabb-Kangas, & M.E. Torres-Guzmán (Eds.), *Imagining multilingual schools: Languages in education and glocalization* (pp. 91-110). Bristol, UK: Multilingual Matters.

McKay, S.L., & Wong, S.C. (Eds.). (2000). *New immigrants in the United States.* Cambridge, UK: Cambridge University Press.

National Center for Education Statistics. (2016a). *Public high school graduation rates.* Washington, DC: U.S. Department of Education. Retrieved from https://nces.ed.gov/programs/coe/indicator_cge.asp

National Center for Education Statistics. (2016b). *Racial/ethnic enrollment in public schools.* Washington, DC: U.S. Department of Education. Retrieved from: https://nces.ed.gov/programs/coe/indicator_cge.asp

Nazario, S. (2014). *Enrique's journey.* New York: Random House.

Perry, S. (2013, January). The bilingual brain. *Society for Neuroscience.* Retrieved from http://www.brainfacts.org/sensing-thinking-behaving/language/articles/2008/the-bilingual-brain

Simons, G.F., & Fennig, C.D. (Eds.). (2017). *Ethnologue: Languages of the world, 20th edition.* Dallas, TX: SIL International. Retrieved from http://www.ethnologue.com/statistics/size

Stewart, D.W. (1993). *Immigration and education: The crisis and the opportunities.* New York: Macmillan.

Thomas, W.P., & Collier, V.P. (2002). *A national study of school effectiveness for language minority students' long-term academic achievement.* Santa Cruz, CA: Center for Research on Education, Diversity and Excellence, University of California-Santa Cruz.

Thomas, W.P., & Collier, V.P. (2009). *English learners in North Carolina, 2009.* Fairfax, VA: George Mason University. A research report provided to the North Carolina Department of Public Instruction.

Thomas, W.P., & Collier, V.P. (2012). *Dual language education for a transformed world*. Albuquerque, NM: Dual Language Education of New Mexico-Fuente Press. Print and electronic editions. Spanish edition in press (2017).

Thomas, W.P., & Collier, V.P. (2014). *English learners in North Carolina dual language programs: Year 3 of this study: School Year 2009-2010*. Fairfax, VA: George Mason University. A research report provided to the North Carolina Department of Public Instruction.

Thomas, W.P., Collier, V.P., & Collier, K. (2010). *English learners in North Carolina, 2010*. Fairfax, VA: George Mason University. A research report provided to the North Carolina Department of Public Instruction.

Thonis, E.W. (1994). Reading instruction for language minority students. In C.F. Leyba (Ed.), *Schooling and language minority students* (2nd ed., pp. 165-202). Los Angeles: Evaluation, Dissemination and Assessment Center, California State University-Los Angeles.

U.S. Department of Education: Office of English Language Acquisition. (2015). *Dual language education programs: Current state policies and practices.* Washington, DC: U.S. Department of Education.

Valdés, G. (2001). *Learning and not learning English: Latino students in American schools.* New York: Teachers College Press.

Valdés, G., Menken, K., & Castro, M. (Eds.). (2015). *Common core bilingual and English language learners: A resource for educators.* Philadelphia: Caslon.

Valenzuela, A. (1999). *Subtractive schooling: U.S.-Mexican youth and the politics of caring.* Albany, NY: State University of New York Press.

Wiley, T.G., Lee, J.S., & Rumberger, R.W. (Eds.). (2009). *The education of language minority immigrants in the United States.* Bristol, UK: Multilingual Matters.

Willis, J. (2012). Bilingual brains—smarter and faster. *Psychology Today.* Retrieved from https://www.psychologytoday.com/blog/radical-teaching/201211/bilingual-brains-smarter-faster

Wolfram, W., & Christian, D. (1989). *Dialects and education: Issues and answers.* Englewood Cliffs, NJ: Prentice Hall Regents.

Wong Fillmore, L. (1991). Second language learning in children: A model of language learning in social context. In E. Bialystok (Ed.), *Language processing in bilingual children* (pp. 49-69). Cambridge: Cambridge University Press.

Index

A

Academic
  achievement *ix, 1, 13–14, 32, 46–48, 57–63, 72*
  language proficiency *26, 45–47*
Accountability/assessment *12–13, 22–23, 27, 30, 44, 68–69, 72*
Achievement gap/closure *1–4, 13–15, 22–23, 26–27, 46–48, 59–61*
Acquisition
  bidialectal *28, 40, 62*
  first language *5–7, 23, 31, 34–35, 39–41, 45, 47–53*
  natural language *7, 39–45*
  second language *6–7, 21–23, 31–34, 39–47, 51–54, 56*
  stages *40–44, 51–54*
Administration/Administrators/principals *ix, x, xi, 11–15, 28, 65, 67–73*

B

Bilingualism
  additive *6, 14, 49–51, 57*
  subtractive *6, 50–51*
Bilinguals
  sequential *52*
  simultaneous *51*
Biliteracy Seal *19, 20*

C

Canadian immersion program *20*
Castañeda v. Pickard *4*
Cognitive
  development *4–9, 14, 23–24, 31, 34–35, 49–52, 61*
  threshold *31, 34, 50–52*
Cost-effectiveness *25, 30, 73*
Cross-cultural competence *25, 57, 62*

D

Dual language curricula *50, 65*
Dual language education
  50:50 program model *8, 21–24*
  90:10 program model *8–9, 20, 48–49*
  one-way *2, 19–20, 25–26, 46*
  two-way *2, 17, 19, 22–27, 46, 57, 65*
  well-implemented program *14, 68, 74*
Dual language programs *1–4, 6, 12, 14, 17–18, 21–27, 30, 35–37, 55–58, 60–63, 67–75*
Dual language schooling *ix, x, xi, 1–4, 7–9, 13–14, 17, 32, 55–57, 65, 72, 75*

E

Engagement, student *10–11, 13–14, 50, 72*
English as a second language/ESL *23, 29–30, 41–48, 53, 71, 73*
English-only *2, 5, 6, 8, 10, 11, 12, 17, 21, 22, 72*
  classroom/instruction *10–11*
  movement *6, 17, 21–22*
  programs *2, 5, 72*
Enrichment *13, 17, 22, 71*
Equal protection *4, 15*

F

Families/parents *ix, x, xi, 4, 6, 17–19, 21, 29, 31–37, 40, 44, 48–52, 57–59, 70, 72*

H

Houston Independent School District *27, 61*

I

Inclusion *23–24, 65*

L

Language
  academic *45–47*
  social *45–46*
Language acquisition (see Acquisition)
Lau v. Nichols *4*
Literacy/biliteracy *8–9, 35, 47–49*
Longitudinal studies/research *1–5, 7, 9, 14, 21–22, 26–27, 33–34, 48, 59–63*

M

Myths *31*

N

North Carolina *10, 19–20, 27, 61–64, 72*

O

Oregon *2–3, 14, 20*
    Woodburn School District *2–3, 26, 29*

P

Parents (see Families/parents)
Pullout *23–24, 65, 75*

R

Reform, school system *9, 12–14, 67, 71–72*

S

School board *xi, 12, 15, 17, 68*
School district *4, 12–13, 19, 22, 25, 29–30, 67–72*
Social
    isolation *23, 25, 65*
    and cultural processes *55–65*
    and emotional support *32–33, 45, 55–57, 64*
Socioeconomic status/background *13–14, 29, 52, 59–60*
Students
    African American *10, 27–28, 61–62*
    English learners *1–8, 10, 13–14, 21–26, 29–30, 42, 46–49, 51, 60, 72*
    native English speakers *1–3, 10, 14–15, 17–22, 47–51, 60–61*
    Hispanic/Latino *1–3, 14, 26–27, 37, 59*
    immigrants *6, 17, 21, 27, 36, 47–48, 50, 53, 57–59*
    Indigenous *18, 29*
    refugees *58*
    with exceptionalities/special needs *1, 5–6, 23, 37, 62–64*

T

Teaching practices
    cooperative learning *9–10, 24, 46, 74–75*
    dual language innovations *28–29, 74–75*
    second language teaching strategies *8–11, 24–27, 59–60, 74–75*
    team teaching *11–12, 23–26, 72–73*
Transfer
    knowledge *9, 13, 47*
    language *6–7, 9, 13, 47*
    literacy *8, 48*
Transitional bilingual education *2, 21–22, 29, 46–47, 65*

U

Utah *19–20*

About the Authors

Professors Wayne Thomas and Virginia Collier are internationally known for their research on long-term school effectiveness for linguistically and culturally diverse students. Dr. Thomas is a professor emeritus of evaluation and research methodology, and Dr. Collier is a professor emerita of bilingual/multicultural/ESL education, both of George Mason University. This is their fourth title in a series published by DLeNM and Fuente Press, following *Educating English Learners for a Transformed World, Dual Language Education for a Transformed World,* and *Creating Dual Language Schools for a Transformed World: Administrators Speak.* For other publications by Dr. Thomas and Dr. Collier, please visit their website at *www.thomasandcollier.com.*